Foreword

Roy Blount Jr.

Okay, let's say the President has accidentally appointed Reese Witherspoon to the Council on Foreign Relations. Or research reveals the flight of the bumblebee to be an optical illusion. Or the governor of Idaho has announced a program to "eradicate the fine arts. Fire ants—whatever."

Whoa, Idahoans! I don't mean to suggest that your state has ever, in fact, had an excess of fire ants, or fine arts. This is all hypothetical. (I can't help noticing, however, that yours is one of the few states boasting not a single station where the program of which I am about to speak is heard each weekend. Hello, Pocatello? So no wonder you can't tell what's hypothetical.)

What I am saying is this:

The staff of *Wait, Wait . . . Don't Tell Me!*, the

National Public Radio weekly news quiz show, will have that story. And it won't be hypothetical. It will be actual stuff that happened.

How do they do it?

We are not supposed to know. When I say "we," I embrace a great mass of humanity. Comprising three main groups:

• Those of us who—by virtue of our regularity and willingness to wear unsterilized public earphones—are privileged to serve as regular panelists on the show. You will find portraits of the most regular of us within these pages: Sue "The Thinking Man's Crumpet" Ellicott. The blithesome, song-improvising prodigy, Adam Felber. The globe-trotting party animal known as P. J. O'Rourke. The sports-and-classic-rock-imbued, hyper-paronomasiac, Charlie Pierce. That sultriest of polymaths, Roxanne Roberts. And I, whom you may know by my nom de plume, J. D. Salinger, or the name I used to wrestle under, Crazy Guggenheim.

• Those distinguished persons—from walks of life entailing at least the occasional stretch limousine—who consent to appear on the program as "Not My Job" guests. Actual examples include not only all the greatest names of NPR but also former Secretary of State Madeline Albright, feline song stylist Eartha Kitt, maverick Senator John McCain, persecuted babe-magnet novelist Salman Rushdie, Arizona Diamondbacks General Manager Joe Garagiola Jr., Zippy the Pinhead creator Bill Griffiths, and blues legend Buddy Guy. All of whom gave first-rate radio, but do you know which one was, intentionally, the funniest? You got it: Maddie.

• And last but not least, those of you out there who—by virtue of your interesting occupation (kelp sorting, licensed necromancy, ursine electrolysis, anything involving underwear), or your engaging salt-of-the-earth vocal quality, or your questionable financial relationship with Executive Producer Doug Berman—may be chosen as Listener Contestants.

We, in sum, who will be asked questions about just such breaking news items as those above. Or say the latest thing in Finland, for cats, is herring-fed mice. Or vice-versa.

wait, wait... don't tell me!®

The Oddly Informative News Quiz

Foreword by
Roy Blount Jr.

RODALE

© 2002 by National Public Radio, Inc.

NPR, npr, National Public Radio, and Wait, Wait . . . Don't Tell Me! are service marks of National Public Radio, Inc. and may not be used without permission of NPR.

Printed in the United States of America
Rodale Inc. makes every effort to use acid-free ∞, recycled paper ♻.

Cover Designer: Christopher Rhoads
Caricature Illustrator: Elizabeth Brandt

Library of Congress Cataloging-in-Publication Data

Wait, wait...don't tell me! : the oddly informative news quiz / foreword by Roy Blount, Jr.
    p.   cm.
  ISBN 1–57954–653–6 paperback
  1. Quiz shows. 2. Wait, wait...don't tell me! (Radio program)
3. National Public Radio (U.S.) 4. Radio scripts. 5. Radio
programs—United States. 6. American wit and humor.
  GV1507.Q5 W35   2002
  791.44'6—dc21   2002009256

Distributed to the book trade by St. Martin's Press

2 4 6 8 10 9 7 5 3 1   paperback

Visit us on the Web at www.rodalestore.com, or call us toll-free at (800) 848-4735.

WE **INSPIRE** AND **ENABLE** PEOPLE TO IMPROVE
THEIR LIVES AND THE WORLD AROUND THEM

Contents

We cannot know whence cometh these questions, we are told, because too much is riding on our answers. Panelists and Not My Job personages risk our/their good names. For you Listener Contestants, the stakes are far higher: If you answer at least two out of three questions correctly, you will win Carl Kassell's voice on your telephone answering machine. (Carl's voice takes many forms. You may select his dead-on impression of Charles de Gaulle saying, "I'm not here right now," or his sly take-off on Joey Buttafuoco singing "The Sound of the Tone" to the tune of "La donna e mobile." On the air, in the "Who's Carl This Time?" segment, Carl has proved himself capable of every conceivable vocal tour de force except one: his rendition of "Fever," the week Peggy Lee passed away, didn't really sound a *lot* like Peggy Lee. Or like "Fever." Or, at any rate, like Peggy doing "Fever" when she was alive. But then Peggy could never really do Carl, either.) If you answer one or fewer correctly . . . you will go through life knowing that you could have had Carl Kassell's voice on your telephone answering machine (with or without the popular telemarketer-repellant whoops) but you don't.

Perhaps, if you took on the *Wait Wait* Limerick Challenge, you were unable to come up with a name in the news that rhymes with "yo' mama been noddin'." Or if Bluff the Listener was your segment, perhaps you ventured a guess that Charlie's story about rabid geese in Kenosha, Wisconsin, was the real one, when instead it was Sue's about bulimic voles in Buggershaftonsbury (Busby), United Kingdom, or Adam's about manic-depressive chickadees on the Cross-Bronx Expressway.

If we were ever to discover, for instance, that there is a Web site devoted entirely to the latest news in unwanted ear-hair—or that the International Criminal Mastermind Association of the World (WIMCA) puts out a weekly newsletter warning its members against state-of-the-art missteps such as attempting to knock over doughnut shops with police cars parked out front—or that Dr. Ervats Porque's *Der Omnitome de la Tutti Boobii* (*All You Need to Know About Boobs in Every Sense*) is now out in translation—we would be able . . .

Let us not mince words. We would be able to cheat. To look up the answers ahead of time.

Which we would do. Yes. We would. As Lauren Bacall once said when the Shah of Iran told her she danced divinely, "You bet your ass, Shah."

Maybe P. J. wouldn't, because he is a Republican. Maybe Roxanne wouldn't, because she can trot up all that stuff in advance anyway from assiduous daily perusal of her principal employer, the *Washington Post.* (And then she scribbles it all down in code, is my suspicion, on Carl's handy French cuffs.) But I'll tell you one thing, Bubba (I use the term, as ever, non-gender-specifically): I would.

Okay, Roxanne would win anyway. Hardly an evening goes by, after all, that she is not out foxtrotting with cool coquettish ear to the feverishly loosened lips of key politicos. (She is the only person other than Strom Thurmond who has ever run fingers through Trent Lott's hair. And Senator Thurmond did it accidentally.) But still. I would do *whatever it takes* to avoid been exposed as unhip to what Jesse Ventura said this week to the Ban the Chokehold Movement, or what the official FAA abbreviation for Swaziland's airport is (DETH), or who, who, who in point of historical fact (rock scholars have just determined) wrote The Book of Love. (Neil Sadaka's sister-in-law, Shana, 1956.)

Because you know why? Because when I *don't* know, Peter Sagal, the Unamuno of Who Knows, the Ionesco of Let's Go, the nimble dramatist-cum-quizmeister about whom they say what they used to say of Sophocles: He has seen life steady, and seen it whole . . .

That Peter. Who by definition knows everything. Off the top of his head. (Not an allusion to his baldness.) Peter Sagal, who studied Tragic Inflection under someone who studied under someone who studied under John Wilkes Booth, will emit an all-but-unvoiced catch of the breath whose import is unmistakable. And a million tuners-in will perceive that when it comes to knowing what Nomar Garciaparra or the flax farmers of Tadzhikistan have been up to this week, I am a cabbagehead.

That's right, a million. This program that began in 1998 with an audience of, I don't know, seventeen, now has over a million listeners, all of whom are cognizant that when called upon to identify the week's top-grossing film in Dar-es-Salaam, I will inevitably commence to snuffle and whine.

And Peter will throw the question open to Charlie, who will not only know the answer but will know that Mordecai "Three-Finger" Brown knew it before he jumped to the Federal League back in Nineteen-Aught-Eleven. Or to Adam, who will spin his answer into a spur-of-the-moment hip-hop operetta. Or to Sue, who will know it, fetchingly, in English. Spot-on.

And the next day I will get e-mails from Rod Abid, Robert Neuhaus, Lorna White, Diantha Parker, Amanda Gibson, Mike Danforth, Philip Goedicke, Manoli Wetherell, Blinky Lightsman, and all those other wonderful people who, if they had not been preoccupied with performing more vital functions off-microphone, would have known the answer, too.

Hey, some of those people (don't ask me which ones, they won't tell us) *write* the questions, in the first place. Okay? So no wonder they know. If I *wrote* the questions, I might well know the answers myself. Because I would presumably have access to the *Complete Works of Yakov Smirnoff*, Paul Wolfowitz's black bag, Gillian Anderson's daily cutting-edge thong briefing, ephemera.net, all the bound volumes of *Crawdaddy*, out-takes from *The Man Show*, Jewel's secret Blog site, *The Week's Top Ten New Sub-Atomic Particles Illustrated*, the Carlyle Corporation's eyes-only pipeline, and *The Bulletin of the Academy of Old TV*.

But this is not all about me. I believe every human who may some day be asked a question on *Wait, Wait . . . Don't Tell Me!* has the inalienable right to keep abreast of this body of knowledge daily, even hourly. A fully informed electorate is. . . . Okay, I take your point. The more fully informed the electorate, the more fully dumbfounded, perhaps. But if we can't have comprehension, or congressmen with pupils in their eyes, we can have answers to (hypothetical) questions like "A hope chest containing a black ten-gallon hat, two pearl-handled six-shooters and a pair of _____ has been traced to the late Søren Kierkegaard."

Answer: woolly chaps. Personally, I prefer deeper questions, like "What is truth?" Preferably multiple-choice. Of course, I never miss "Walter Scott's Personality Parade," and because I paid such good attention in ninth-grade science (the only class in which I didn't sit behind Bitsy Bloodworth, who smelled like peaches), I know more than the average lay person about the properties of zinc. I've got answers enough, in short, to hold my own at A-list swap meets and shrimp festivals. But not enough to satisfy the seething curiosity of the minds behind *Wait Wait*. Still I beat on, my boat against the current, borne back ceaselessly into the Lightning Round.

It is too late for me. The whole world already knows that I was perhaps the last to know that, say, Andy Griffith and Yanni together have cut a techno-pop album. I am too tarnished to lead a popular uprising. So the ball is in your court. Hitch up your britches, boot up your laptops, log onto www.npr.org, and before you know it you will have linked—lunk?—your way to the *Wait Wait* Discussion Board. There, you may make *your* voice heard, so to speak. Seize the moment. Demand what is not within public radio's purview to withhold. You need to know where this stuff comes from. The siren voice of Carl is calling.

Or if you have a life or something, you could just listen to the show.

Preface

Peter Sagal

Historians may be debating the exact date for years, but a rough consensus is already emerging: Truth, finally, became stranger than fiction in or about January 1998, when reports emerged of the President having an affair with a White House intern who looked strangely like Jason Alexander's love child. We don't know if was a coincidence, or a sign from an approving God, but 1 week before the world heard the name Lewinski for the first time, they (or, at least, the listeners of the 12 or so radio stations that first carried our show) heard *Wait, Wait . . . Don't Tell Me!*, the NPR News Quiz.

Like the rest of NPR, we at *Wait, Wait* are dedicated to bringing you the most accurate reporting on the issues and events of the day. Unlike the rest of NPR, we bring it to you because we think it's hilarious. Everybody else says: Be informed, be aware, be involved. We say: Can you believe these people? or Isn't that amazing? He ate the entire donkey!

This book is a compendium of stories we plucked from newspapers, Web sites, wire services, NPR and other public radio broadcasts, TV, magazines, and other, actual, bona-fide news sources, the kind that employ fact checkers and editors and worry about libel suits. Everything on our show, and in this book, is true, as far as we know. As proof, we offer the simple fact: We could never make this stuff up. We're smart and funny people, but in terms of generating laughs, we are in awe of the clueless politicians, peculiar animals, addled pop stars, idiotic would-be criminals, and all the rest who seem to be out there every week making sure we'll have a solid hour of material come the weekend. It is they, dear reader, not we, who are the authors of this book.

Each radio show focuses on news from that week, but this book organizes the questions into various categories, so that, say, the dumb-criminal fetishists among you can skip directly to that chapter. The answers are to be found in the back of the book, but as tempting as it might be to check your best guesses against the unbelievable truth, we suggest lingering back there. Serving a rather discriminating audience, we understand that they don't merely want to know that a Georgia legislator introduced a bill banning answering the door naked; they want to know why. Actually, why she did that is anybody's guess, but you can find the official explanation on page 65.

On the radio show, we presented this material in a few different ways. Some stories we presented as straightforward questions to our panel. Others were quotations re-enacted by co-host and scorekeeper Carl Kasell, with the listeners trying to identify the quotation's speaker or subject. Still others were multiple-choice questions about abstruse topics, posed to our Celebrity Guests. (Our Celebrities get the advantage of multiple choice because, as will be clear from this book, Celebrities in general tend not to be too bright.) And, in our "Bluff" segment, our panelists presented our listeners with three news stories in the same category: Only one of them was real. Your job, of course, is to pick the real story. On our show, listeners who call in and successfully answer our questions are rewarded with Carl Kasell's voice on their home answering machine. I wish we could provide that service to each and every one of you readers, because, after all, all the listeners did was call a toll-free number, and you actually had to shell out 10 bucks. But Carl only has so many hours in the day, you know, and besides, if everybody has one, what happens to Carl's cachet?

Still, we encourage you to treat this book not so much as a compendium of trivia but as a test. Consider each question carefully: If you don't know, discuss it with your friends, or if you have no friends, with your fellow EverQuest players. Then, take your best guess, and check your answer at the end of the book. If you got it wrong—and believe me, you will most of the time, because most of this stuff surpasseth human understanding—marvel at the strangeness of the world we live in. If you get a question right, congratulate yourself, because you are truly a worldly philosopher. If you get them all right, bub, you've got a problem.

Enjoy.
Peter Sagal
Host, *WWDTM*

Animals

There's nothing we love more than animals. They can be wild, cute, fluffy, bald, newborn, or dead. We love them all. Insects or mammals. Reptiles or birds. Hey, even fossils. Why? Because they can't complain. We can say pretty much anything we like about an animal and get away with it. We could easily ask questions about other non-complainers, such as fruits or vegetables, but why bother? You can only go so far with "rutabaga" or "parsnip" as a punch line. Besides, next thing you know, we'd get carnivores baying for matching jokes about gizzards and oxtail.

Without animal questions, Roxanne probably would win every show. She'd ace every question from Washington politics to celebrity gossip and the rest of us would have to go home. The way things are, the

intro by
Sue
Ellicott

Beyond-the-Beltway panelists at least have a slim hope each week of glory, if only because the animal answers are usually so off the wall you're best off guessing. How else could we know about parrots that make 911 calls, hamster races in England, or deer that fall into people's tubs while couples are bathing? It helps to be up on nature, of course. So if you went to the zoo a lot as a kid, you're in good shape. I didn't, but I did have pet rabbits, guinea pigs, a cat called Bedsocks, gerbils, a hamster, and a box of spiders. Roy lives in the country, so he's okay. Adam's a Brooklyn man, but he does all right on the pigeon questions. Frankly, it's often occurred to me that the writers could be making up some of the animal stuff. But even if they are, who's going to sue? A slandered squirrel? A libeled llama?

Weird Wild Kingdom

Limerick

1) Although we are going full throttle,
It seems that we penguins just dawdle.
But this clumsy gait
Is ideal for our weight
And that's why we walk with a _____.

2) I've got short, stumpy arms like a shrimp.
And my legs hurt, I walk with a limp.
I'm not king of my place
Don't kick sand in my face
I'm less T-Rex and more of a _____.

Answers on Pgs. 111–112

3) These taxiderm's won't be rebuffed.
I caved in when they just barely puffed.
I feel like a schnook.
My fish's fresh on the hook
And I'm pressured to have my catch _____.

4) The Miami Seaquarium conducted an investigation after some employees _____ an endangered turtle.

5) In Texas, a grandma was run over by a _____.

6) A cock-crowing contest in New Mexico was ruined when the birds were _____.

Pick One 7) It's a sign of an affluent society to have domestic pets and companion animals. It's the sign, perhaps, of a declining society to have professionals who are paid to provide those pets with horoscopes. What used to be "obedience training" is now "pet behavior modification," and there are people out there who'll sell you various products to help you do it. Which of these is actually available to help you make your companion animal even more companionable?

A) The Kitty Climber, a set of two Velcro pads which, when attached to a cat's front claws, will result in the cat helplessly climbing up the couch instead of scratching it

B) The Aboistop, a device which automatically sprays a distracting scent in front of a dog's nose whenever it barks

C) The Shoe Surprise, a device which, when placed in a shoe, emits a horrible noise when chewed, thereby curing dogs of that habit

Limerick

8) I work out in the pool of my gym.
But not 'cause I want to be trim.
If I can't evade ships
I'll be served up with chips.
I'm a cod that must learn how to _____.

9) Davy Crockett confronts Daniel Boone,
"Don't this make you feel like a goon?
With these empty traps
They'll feast on our caps.
We can't seem to snare a _____."

10) I was chasing my own bottom half;
Then I caught it, now that was a gaffe.
With my mouth on my tail,
My friends start to wail.
See, it's easy to make a dog _____.

11) The Longhorn moos, "For goodness' sake!
There's more than just sirloin to take.
Come on, try your luck
Right under the chuck."
They've discovered a new cut of _____.

Fill in the Blank

12) A construction company in Florida used rock music to drive away _____.

13) A veterinarian in Xenia, Ohio, is being sued by _____.

Answers on Pgs. 112–114

14) In recognition for valiantly foiling a robbery attempt, Minneapolis police have given an award to _____.

15) The Environment Minister in Australia wants the state to enact more safety restrictions on tourists after he saw a tape of some visitors _____.

Pick One

16) There are old myths about why mosquitoes seem to bite some people more than others. But most aren't true. In fact, nervous people and people with smelly shoes are among the most likely targets. How do we know this about these stealthy vampiric pests? We looked through the book *Mosquito: A Natural History of Our Most Persistent and Deadly Foe* by Andrew Spielman and Michael D'Antonio. According to the book, a Canadian power station suffered repeated malfunctions until it was discovered that the machinery was being gummed up by thousands upon thousands of dead mosquitoes. What attracted the mosquitoes to their untimely doom?

A) The plant's equipment produced a high-pitched whine that was remarkably similar to the sound of a certain kind of female mosquito, luring legions of male mosquitoes to their doom.

B) The air intake had been placed near a medical waste facility whose blood bags made it a popular site for mosquitoes of all kinds.

C) The plant's "doughnut table Tuesday" caused an unusually high blood sugar level in employees, which mosquitoes for miles around could detect.

17) *Mosquito* also suggests that during World War II, one of the reasons for the U. S. success in the Pacific was the rigorous anti-mosquito measures ordered by General Douglas MacArthur. Which of the following is an actual anti-mosquito propaganda campaign from the war?

A) Cartoons and posters featuring the characters Malaria Moe and Anopheles Ann

B) The song parody "Yellow Fever," set to the tune of the standard "Fever" and heavily featured on military radio stations

C) An Army-mandated burlesque sketch during USO shows, in which a soldier is lured out of his protective clothing by a beautiful bombshell who turns out to be a mosquito in disguise

Limerick

18) The stallion chews through his reviews.
"Though I should make them snooze, they enthuse!
I take my sweet time
And I don't make a dime.
But they love me 'cause I always _____."

19) The octopus often alarms
When trying to work all his charms.
"Oh, honey, be kind.
I do love your mind.
That's why I am groping your _____."

20) For my neighborhood's young kennel lodgers,
I'm smoother than newscasting codgers.
Can you say "hoochie cooch?"
Oh, I knew you could, pooch.
Dogs get pillow talk from Mister _____.

Answers on Pgs. 114–115

21) A house fire that caused $100,000 in damage in Grand Chute, Wisconsin, is being blamed on the couple's _____.

22) In Boston, a _____ was selected for jury duty.

23) Here are three stories of how the natural world is mirroring our wanton ways. One is real, but two, thank goodness, are monstrosities rejected, so far, by our Mother Earth. It's up to you to guess the real one.

A) Nutria, the fat little swamp rodents that live in the Louisiana Bayou, have taken to walking en masse along the bicycle trails in the Huey P. Long National Forest near New Iberia. Scientists believe that the nutria have discovered the bike paths are a safer way to get from one rich feeding ground to another without having to worry about alligators and other aquatic predators. Also, researchers say, the nutria have come to realize that bicycles pose a lesser threat than cars and trucks they would encounter on paved roads. Three tourists already have been injured in bike-rat collisions and officials are contemplating erecting barriers along each side of the trails.

B) As if the gorillas at the San Diego Zoo didn't have enough problems with the subtropical climate and a growing antibiotic tolerance, now they're mixed up in gangs. Zoo officials believe the trouble started when a member of the Lositanos Youth Gang visited the gorillas on a school trip and became fascinated with the zoo's attempts to teach American Sign Language to the gorilla population, which is the largest in North America. The unidentified gang member soon succeeded in teaching several gorillas his gang sign, or greeting. Soon, members of Lositanos were regular visitors to the gorilla habitat and at least two other gangs had succeeded in teaching gorillas their signs. Startlingly, this has led to problems—two male gorillas squared off, one flashing the Lositanos sign, and the other flashing the sign for the San Diego Crips. Neither gorilla would back down, forcing the zoo to separate them before violence ensued.

C) Ornithologists say that several different bird species in Australia are calling each other with calls that sound suspiciously like cell phone rings. Australia is one of the world's leaders in cell phone use and as a result, the melodic chirping of mobile phones has reached the ears of at least six varieties of so-called mimic birds. Mimic birds imitate sounds found in nature, like other bird calls, but have also been recorded impersonating things like cameras and chain saws. Gregory Czechura, a bird expert at the Queensland Museum, says that cell phone mimics are mostly males looking for mates, perhaps inspired by one another. "It means there is a male that is up-to-date, on-the-ball and has the latest sounds," he says.

Limerick

24) The crab hobbles off with a limp.
"That's not a stromatopod wimp.
He punched out the lamprey
Quick! Cook him in scampi
Be careful who you call a _____."

25) The judge said, "Let's make one thing clear:
The B. S. will stop now and here.
Good bovine aesthetics
Don't need no cosmetics.
Now, please take that wig off your _____."

26) On the phone, the zookeeper goes limp.
"Stop your wheezing and snuffling, you imp!
Say something. Speak!
Wait, I know that shriek.
These prank calls have come from our _____."

Answers on Pgs. 115–116

27) I need me a trout with more brawn.
The scrawny ones just make me yawn.
To attract better mates
No eggs drop on first dates.
See, I'm only pretending to _____.

28) Oh, Canada has few believers
In dam-building overachievers.
Our national symbol
Is simply too nimble.
We're pelted by too many _____.

Pick One **29)** We spent some time relaxing with *The Ants*, the monumental book on the little critters by Bert Hölldobler and Edward O. Wilson, and we're just swimming with ant trivia. Ants do a lot of things that we thought were the exclusive domain of people. Which of these things have ant colonies been observed doing in the wild?

A) Attending sporting events

B) Capturing and keeping slaves

C) Shopping peacefully with other species at large ant malls

30) Some kinds of ants are fierce warriors and are constantly attacking other species of ants and insects, so some have developed remarkable military abilities. Which of these is a real ant?

A) *Dorylus scholnicki*, which swallows tiny seeds, then fires them through its nose at enemies

B) *Camponotus saundersi*, which maneuvers itself close to the enemy and then blows itself up

C) *Paltothyreus albrightsis*, which runs up into trees above enemy nests, drops nuts on them, and then runs home

31) Zookeepers in Michigan were embarrassed when a _____ made a successful dash for freedom and ran away.

32) Part of an Illinois family's house was severely damaged after their dog tried to _____.

33) The musical world of Eastern Australia was recently turned on its head with some new tunes sung by _____.

34) Despite a serious scientific inquiry into the subject, no evidence has been found to prove that penguins _____.

35) The hardest thing about having a pet of course, is that pets don't live as long as we do. Which of these services is now available to grieving pet lovers?

A) Video pet simulation, in which videographers create a video—taped pre-mortem, of course—of the pet playing and eating, which can then be played on an endless loop on a television

Answers on Pgs. 116–118

B) E-mails from pet heaven, in which a company will intermittently send an owner fond messages, presumably from beyond the grave

C) Freeze-drying, whereby a taxidermist can quickly preserve your pet in a lifelike pose, for example, sleeping or resting by your bed

36) In Italy, contestants train for an annual mosquito-related competition that has proved surprisingly popular. What is the contest?

A) The Sweet Skin Championships, in which nearly naked contestants munch bananas, spray perfume, and sweat profusely in an attempt to garner the most mosquito bites in a 1-hour period.

B) *Il Festo del Probo*, a summer celebration with a mosquito theme that offers prizes for the most realistic, frightening, and amusing mosquito costumes.

C) The mosquito-killing championships, where competitors wearing swimsuits and socks have 5 minutes each to squash as many mosquitoes as possible with their bare hands.

Limerick

37) Captain Nemo, we just have got rid
Of the monster that stands for your Id.
But, no, I am sorry,
You can't have calamari.
We've pickled the gigantic _____.

38) We bray at the screen, but we're on key.
Still the cars at the drive-in get honky.
They say, "Move that mule!"
But we broke no rule.
Besides, she's no mule, she's a _____.

39) When Mickey dropped down upon his knee,
I thought, "He's proposing now, isn't he?"
But he squeaked, "Shh, don't talk.
And watch out for the hawk.
They're hunting the rodents at _____."

40) A mail carrier in Newtonville, Massachusetts, de-manded action after being regularly attacked on his route by a ferocious _____.

41) Dolphins have been discovered to be able to _____ in the mirror.

42) Oh, jeez, see this thin, scrawny bod?
He's no good for lutefisk, Maude.
I've caught him too often,
My heart starts to soften.
I think I'll retire this _____.

43) The young matador weaves with great flair
But he dreads being caught unaware.
"To avoid more close shaves
I'll learn how he behaves,
Which I'll judge by the bull's facial _____."

Answers on Pgs. 118–119

44) Tippi Hedren knew just how it goes.
We swoop down and peck at your nose.
From Hitchcock's dark urges
To Tokyo's scourges.
We're violent, scavenging _____.

Pick One   **45) Ants have evolved some very tricky ways to survive over the years. Which of these is the way a real Malaysian ant species manages to get by?**

A) When attacked by an anteater, the colony collectively mimics the sound of a jaguar, scaring the anteater away.

B) When food runs short, they trade virile younger males to other colonies in return for supplies.

C) When the nest gets wet, they drink the water, run outside, pass it, and run back in for more.

Business

Something that we often discuss in the corridors of power at *WWDTM* (okay, it's actually only one corridor, but it does lead to a lovely terrace overlooking Lake Michigan) is how fortunate we were to start our show just as the Clinton presidency began to devolve into the prurient mess of interns, hearings, and self-righteousness. Being there for one of the more ridiculous periods of American political history was indisputably a boon to our fledgling show, even though we panelists soon found ourselves out of ammo once every entendre had been doubled and tripled and still the "case" slogged on.

But there was another, less ballyhooed bit of providence for us as we embarked on our journey: We were there to witness the dot-com bubble at its most ludicrously overinflated, with its bottomless venture capital and inexplicably successful startups that didn't even have to bother with purchasing smoke machines or mirrors for their smoke-and-mirrors presentations.

When the bubble burst, it proved to be a piñata full of stories for us as well. As the offices began to clear out and investors started demanding business plans that made at least passing reference to "making money," we at *WWDTM* got to wonder at the ruins of these short-lived empires. Of course, it wasn't all cake and ice cream for us humorists. Making fun of people getting rich comes across as petty and jealous, and poking fun at people getting poor seems cruel and spiteful. But we always have our standbys—our own Wait Wait 500, if you will.

There will always be a Microsoft, crab-walking its way to world domination; the Cult of Greenspan is going strong, the markets laying offerings upon the altar at His slightest facial tic; and—most important—millionaires and billionaires will continue to be wacky, and to do so in big, big ways. Bless them.

Capitalist Fools

Bluff News Story 1) In these days of Home Depot, Walgreens, and Wal-Mart, you might think that the family business is dead and gone. No more kindly man in an apron serving you pickles just like his father did and his father before him. But wait! We're going to give you three stories of a family business being revived. One story is true, but the other two are no more real than, say, Betty Crocker. Your job is to tell us which one is the real story.

A) If it's Massachusetts, it must be The Kennedys. Walter Laningham, a third cousin to Sargent Shriver and thus at least a part-time Kennedy, has left his seat as a State Representative for Massachusetts and is beginning a career in catfish farming in Mississippi. Laningham announced that he plans to open four restaurants called the New Frontier Fish House and he hopes one day to open one in Hyannis, Massachusetts, not far from the famous family compound. A Kennedy family spokesman commented, "We haven't talked to Walter in some time. I hope his catfish have better taste than he does."

B) Orlando Montague, direct descendant of the Earl of Sandwich, is carrying on family tradition via his new sandwich delivery business called The Earl of Sandwich, which delivers freshly made hoagies and the like to locations in central London. The fourth Earl of Sandwich just slapped some beef and bread together so he wouldn't have to stop playing cards, but Montague is eager to establish sandwich excellence using only the best ingredients. "There are 250 years of expectation on us," Montague said Monday in his kitchen. "We have tremendous pressure on us to get this right." His father, the eleventh Earl of Sandwich and company president, agrees, adding that, "The true test is to be able to hold it in one hand." The Earl of Sandwich received The Earl of Sandwich's first delivery at the House of Lords.

C) Not every Playboy Bunny is blond and giggly—some are blond and fluffy. In a twist on the family business, Christine Hefner, president of Playboy Enterprises and daughter of founder Hugh Hefner, has revived a weakness for rabbits that started when her father gave her a real pet bunny when she was eight years old. Five years ago, Hefner allowed an Illinois rabbit breeder to name a purebred cashmere longhair rabbit Christine, after her. Since then, she's become a breeder of show rabbits as well as a judge and a sponsor at shows in Chicago, New York, and Los Angeles. She's also become a major contributor to the American Humane Society's campaign to rescue pet rabbits abandoned every Easter. "Bunnies have been very good to the Hefner family, both two-legged and four-footed varieties," Hefner joked to reporters. "I'm happy and proud to help when I can."

Answers on Pg. 120

Pick One   2) In addition to coming up with completely new innovations, inventors are also trying to bring digital technology to bear on older devices. Which of these is now available in a fully computerized version?

A) The digital fry pan

B) The digital wheelbarrow

C) The digital sledgehammer

Bluff News Story   3) If you've ever wrangled with an insurance company over a claim, just listen to these three stories of people trying to extend the reach of their insurance umbrellas. One of these valiant efforts is really in the works, but the other two aren't on any claim forms, at least not yet. And it's up to you to guess the real one.

A) Back in 1986, when famously paranoid fiber-optic billionaire Edward Holland retired to his very own island in the South Pacific, it was assumed that he wouldn't be heard from again. But Mr. Holland is back in the news suing his insurance agency for breach of contract on his MIR Space Station insurance policy. Mr. Holland insured his island home for $40 million against "damages incurred from the atmospheric reentry of the MIR." The station crash landed, and though the nearest chunk came only within 200 miles of Mr. Holland's home in the U. S.–Guam Island chain, Holland claims that the fiery crash disrupted TV, satellite, and other vital communications for over an hour, cutting him off from his trading and news about the crash, "causing mental anguish and material monetary loss." The insurance company claims that the policy covered only direct hits, but Mr. Holland is going to get his day in court—provided he's willing to travel the 3,000 miles to get there.

B) Toronto-based journalist Liz Hannigan says the deadlines made her do it. The "it" being daily shipments of chocolate truffles costing around $50

U. S. per pound from La Maison du Chocolat, a renowned Parisian choco-latier with a store on Madison Avenue in New York City. Hannigan, polit-ical columnist for the Toronto *Globe & Mail*, is challenging health-care provider Blue Cross/Blue Shield's refusal to reimburse her for more than 28 pounds of fruit-infused truffles and chocolate-robed pistachio marzi-pans consumed while "under stress during coverage of a Canadian con-stitutional crisis in 1999." "I was depressed," Hannigan writes in her column, "and truffles are definitely cheaper than Prozac or Zoloft."

C) A Pennsylvania state representative is lobbying medical insurance companies to cover toupees, specifically if the hair loss, which occasions the use of the toupee, is caused by a medical condition. "If a toupee is prescribed by a doctor, it seems only fitting that it should be covered, minus the patient's deductible, naturally." The bill stresses that this isn't just a vanity issue, as a head-covering toupee regulates body temperature and shields the delicate skin of the scalp from ultraviolet rays. While the toupee insurance bill is under consideration, the same lawmaker has in-troduced a companion bill that would make toupees sales tax- exempt.

Fill in the Blank

4) 7-11's Big Gulp expanded until it was bigger than _____.

5) An AP poll finds that, if given $1,000, more than half of Americans would no longer put it in _____.

Limerick

6) The superstore was a good call, Art.
Convenience plays more than a small part.
The RV is docked
Let's shop 'round the clock
There's nothing like camping at _____.

Pick One   **7) Here's an application of digital technology to an age-old problem, heretofore immune to technological intervention:**

A) The Late-Comers Watch, which gradually speeds up as you approach scheduled appointments, resulting in your arriving early

B) The Snore Stopper, which delivers a mild electric shock when it detects loud snores

C) The Mate Finder, a tiny homing device you can hide in your spouse's wallet, which uses global positioning satellite technology to pinpoint their location at any time

Bluff News Story   **8) The day of the little guy seems to be over, gone with the corner hardware store, the independent coffee shop, and the locally owned newspaper. But we've heard a story of a brave individual throwing down the gauntlet against a huge international power. We'll tell you three uplifting stories about fighting the power, but only one is true. The other two, just wishful thinking.**

A) Lady Doris Morgan of Blackpool, England, is landed gentry, but if her claim is correct, she may be more than that—she may be the real queen of England. Lady Morgan filed a suit asserting that she has discovered documents that prove that she is a direct, legal descendant of King Henry VIII, which would make her a Tudor and gives her higher claim to the throne than Elizabeth and her Hanover line. An issue is whether Henry VIII's third wife, Anne, was married to Henry at the time of her son's conception and birth. Though Henry renounced both the son and the marriage, Lady Morgan claims she can now prove her great-great-great-great-great-great-great-great-great-great-grandfather's legitimacy. Though she acknowledges her chances are slim, Lady Morgan has high hopes for the legal action. She says, "Obviously, I'm not about to storm the palace, and swords and stones are far too scarce these days, but in time, the truth will out."

Answers on Pgs. 120–121

B) In this corner, Yahoo Inc., the billion-dollar Internet company publisher and high-tech giant. And in the other corner, Yahoo Serious, an obscure Australian comedian. Mr. Serious (that's his legal name) says that Yahoo.com, which he's never even heard of until recently, is trying to take advantage of all the goodwill he's created with his hit movies, among them *Young Einstein*, *Reckless Kelly*, and *Mr. Accident*. His lawyer says, "Yahoo Serious had more expert exposure before Yahoo Inc. was even thought of!" Yahoo Inc. had no comment.

C) In the war of convenience stores, it was Flanny & Ward's against Mom 'n' PopCo. And Mom 'n' PopCo braked. In "Ward's Words," his weekly paid-advertisement column in the Quincy, Illinois *New Herald*, Ward Dukart has been taking it to the tri-state chain of quick-stop stores called Mom 'n' Pops. "This soulless corporate entity," wrote Ward, "can render extinct my wife and I, but we have served this community's short-term food needs for 27 years and we'll prevail. The little heads in that Mom 'n' Pop logo aren't anybody. Flanny & Ward's is me and Flanny and in the area of live bait, well, they'll have a vending machine." Last week, after a deluge of angry mail, Mom 'n' PopCo announced it had abandoned plans to open a store right across the road from Flanny & Ward's.

Fill in the Blank

9) The *New York Times* reported that things might in fact be very dire on Wall Street because _____ found in New York's financial district are getting shorter.

10) Dr. Kenneth Cooper, the man who pioneered the idea of "aerobics" and was a candidate to become the Surgeon General, has been discussing _____ as a tangible incentive for people to maintain their health.

11) _____, a company in Michigan, is suing another company with the same name, asserting copyright infringement and lost income due to intentional confusion of customers.

Answers on Pgs. 121–122

Bluff News Story

12) To help us get over the loss of Kosmo.com and Webvan, new players have emerged in the effort to give us opportunities to let someone else do the heavy lifting. Our panelists are going to tell you three stories about the latest in "don't do it yourself schemes." Your job: Pick the real one.

A) For years, The Gap has urged you to fall into it, but now, if you won't come to The Gap, The Gap will come to you. Last week, in San Diego, The Gap launched the first of 50 planned mobile Gap stores dubbed The Gap MORE for Mobile Outlet Retail Store. The store is a 60-foot tractor-trailer that folds out cunningly into, ". . . an attractive retail environment, which displays and stocks all the latest styles." Not only will The Gap MORE position itself at public events and in high traffic areas, but for a fee, you can actually get The Gap to come to where you are. Depending on the time of day, this service can run you between $200 and $500 an hour. But according to a spokesperson, one group of San Diego neighbors has already pooled their resources to have The Gap attend their next barbecue. The Gap says it plans to roll out their next 50 stores by Christmas.

B) The latest product from the WHAM-O people, who gave you the Frisbee and countless other useless diversions, is the Twiddle Master, a device that takes the work out of that most traditional of idle pursuits, twiddling your thumbs. The Twiddle Master is a small cylinder into which a thumb is inserted at each end. Once activated, the Twiddle Master rotates the thumbs in a gentle, circular motion, one over the other. The device can be set for durations of up to a half-hour, and WHAM-O recommends it as a therapeutic to those people suffering from ergonomic injuries suffered on the job. "The Twiddle Master is so relaxing that you hardly know your thumbs are being twiddled at all," commented WHAM-O spokesman Martin Gufflin, which it seems was the point all along.

C) A new British company is promising the unthinkable: an end to waiting in endless lines or queues. The odd British habit of forming orderly lines, even at bus stops, has led to the country's first queuing agency. Statistics show that the British spend about a year of their lives standing in line, and Queue for You promises to save time for busy Londoners—for a price, of course. Queue for You charges 20 pounds (about $29 an hour) and employs about 80 people who will line up for anything, (passports, concerts, you name it, they'll stand for it). Most of the workers are recruited from the ranks of long-term unemployed. "It's a job that doesn't require a lot of skill or experience," explains Patrick Young, director of the agency's parent company, Fifteen Minutes. "All you need is plenty of patience."

Fill in the Blank 13) "The car worked for him, but I only dated him once. He refused to wear the paper bag over his head for another date. But I earned his respect in the fact that I was a 15-year-old girl who could actually handle a four-speed."

That's a woman named Val McClatchey who said she dated the ugliest guy in school because she wanted to drive his _____, which will no longer be made.

14) "It shows that they are looking for the same qualities as any truck buyer: durability and reliability . . ."

That's Wade Hoyt, a spokesman for Toyota, taking pride that the _____ seem to be very big fans of Toyota pickup trucks.

Bluff News Story 15) With the world economy on the skids, shopping has taken on an importance beyond making sure you've got that new combination wine steward/personal humidifier from Hammacher Schlemmer. We have three new ways to entice you back to your local galleria. One is real; two are ideas already relegated to the outlet malls. Your job is to pick the real enticement to shop.

A) Now, you can enjoy the great, wide-open outdoors experience within an easy walk of The Gap. The Mall of America in Bloomington, Minnesota, began its "Camping at the Mall" program last week, and over 1,000 adventurous consumers showed up to "camp out" inside the mall overnight. The event featured piped-in nature sounds, well-tended campfires, and professional sto-rytellers to tell the campers spooky tales. All campers were given cards good for a 10-percent discount on all mall merchandise when the stores opened the next morning. Mall of America event planner Deborah Kalacut says that the overwhelming response to the promotion means that mall camping may become a regular event in a difficult post-Christmas season.

B) Here we come a-wassailing off to Pottery Barn. The Acton Group of Malls in Massachusetts has developed a program through which groups of shoppers can form themselves into cadres of carolers. Going store to store, the carolers are greeted with bargain goods and gift certificates. "It is a great way to instill that holiday spirit, while ensuring visibility for our tenants," said Robert O'Nolan, director of marketing for the Acton Group. On Christmas Eve afternoon at Diamond Square, the flagship mall of the Acton Group, there will be a Dickens-themed Christmas party and the best group of carolers will be awarded $1,000 each to spend any-where they want to in the mall in the last 15 minutes before closing.

C) Okay, blokes, listen up. A mall in Braehead, Scotland, has come up with a solution to an old problem: men who hate shopping. A new service allows women to drop off their hubbies or boyfriends in a so-called "recharge zone" equipped with video games, table football, and certain men's maga-zines. In exchange, the ladies get to shop till they drop with their free male husband or boyfriend stand-in, one that won't whine outside the changing room. The "Dump One, Get One Free" policy, as the mall *isn't* calling its pilot scheme, was launched after a poll found that one in four British men, age 18 to 24, would rather have lunch with their granny than go shopping with their girlfriend. Alan Bryant, age 30, who's working as a surrogate boyfriend/personal shopper, says customers are happy so far. But, it's caveat emptor. When one lady tried on a miniskirt recently, he compli-mented her. "However, she wasn't the skinniest," he said later. "She bought it, and I felt a wee bit guilty about that."

Answers on Pg. 122

Limerick

16) Please start up, we need to go far.
Like the Love Bug, you, too, are a star.
Do you know how it feels
To make deals with your wheels?
I must cope with the moods of my _____.

17) Where's the sideshow for underage snackers?
This penguin seeks corporate backers.
I want to audition
For Barnum's tradition
I'll be the new animal _____.

Fill in the Blank

18) The Hormel company of Austin, Minnesota, has quietly given up its fight to prevent the unauthorized use of _____, a word they say they own.

19) Former South African president Nelson Mandela has stopped a pair of businessmen from using his name to sell _____.

20) According to *USA Today*, every 2 hours, every day in the year, someone, somewhere in this country _____ mega-retailer Wal-Mart.

Bluff News Story

21) In plenty of time for Christmas, we heard about a luxury item that, while previously unknown to *shlubs* like us, is apparently the height of esoteric, expensive taste. We'll describe three luxury products that were new to us . . . one is real, but the other two are just proverbially gilded lilies. And it's up to you to guess the real item.

A) What some connoisseurs consider the very best coffee available retails for about $300 a pound. And it's not because the pickers themselves demand a high wage. The coffee beans are picked, or rather poached, at the height of ripeness by palm civets, which are nocturnal catlike animals native to Indonesia. Described as timid, fruit-loving carnivores, civets swallow the best beans from the coffee fields and then process them as any animal would. The beans are then gathered by humans, washed (presumably very carefully), and then roasted. The result, flavored by the civets' digestive juices and the scent glands in its posterior, makes a rich, complex cup cherished by some, but which one merchant wryly calls, "Good to the last dropping."

B) Forget the chemical peels, acid wraps and mud tubs . . . this year's hot new skin treatment is the cranberry bath. It started last year when Noire Alsidere, the proprietress of the chique Alsidere chain of high-end spas, was vacationing in Maine. She says she was in a restaurant when her waiter used the expression, "As smooth as a bog man's bottom." Further inquiry led to Alsidere's learning the origin of the expression. Apparently, the men who picked cranberries in New England's cranberry bogs were known to maintain soft, youthful skin throughout their lifetimes. After confirming this (Miss Alsidere will not say how), the cranberry bath was born. The total immersion in a tub full of warm, fresh cranberries and a little water does not come cheap. One 20-minute bath will run you about $700. But the rich and famous are lining up for it at Alsidere's spas, and most top spas have followed suit.

C) What's the latest high-status indulgence among folks in the entertainment industry? Illicit socks. That's what they're called by the shadowy outfit that designs and deals them. Because they're made of hemp, a plant closely related to marijuana, they are illegal; that accounts for some of their cachet. But Illicit socks are also extremely fine-spun, sturdily constructed, and precisely measured to fit each foot individually. "I have very sensitive feet," says one studio exec. "Any other sock is agony. But with these, it's like walking on clouds." You can tell genuine Illicits by the logo, a bright red toenail right over the wearer's little toe. The price? Around $200 . . . per sock.

Answers on Pgs. 122–124

Pick One

22) Sony Corporation pulled a series of holiday ads featuring Santa because it was believed it would offend children. Did the ad campaign feature:

A) Santa being kidnapped and tormented by two men who demand that people go to the Sony Web site as a condition of his release

B) Santa blowing up an Aibo robot dog because kids want those for Christmas instead of his elf-made goodies

C) Santa listening to controversial rapper Eminem on his Sony Walkman

Fill in the Blank

23) There's a lot of concern about how the economy is doing, but according to analysts, _____ business does very well in hard times.

24) The Coty Fragrance company is introducing 001, a new perfume that's designed to smell like _____.

25) "From 14 to 40 a woman needs good looks. From 40 to 60, she needs personality. After 60, she needs cash."
That statement of principle came from _____, a woman who died at the age of 83 after providing generations of women with cash, not to mention, on occasion, genuine pink Cadillacs.

26) "He became a benevolent fat-delivery system all his own, living in a universe where every day, people implored [him] to please bring back the Monterey Ranch chicken sandwich or to add more bacon to the bacon double cheeseburger."
That was Hank Steuver in the *Washington Post*, offering an epitaph for _____.

Answers on Pgs. 124–125

Education

intro by
Roxanne
Roberts

We at *Wait Wait* planned to do a comprehensive analysis of modern education, but the dog ate our homework. Then we found a plagiarized dissertation on the Internet for $25, but we already sent out for pizza and beer. So we stayed up all night and came up with this theory, for which we fully expect to get an A or we're suing for grade discrimination. The average person has two distinct encounters with the school system. The first begins in kindergarten and ends with a diploma and a hangover; the main objective is to avoid teachers, homework, and learning as much as possible. The second brush occurs when we walk our precious little geniuses to their first day of school, only to discover in horror that the principal, teachers, and counselors are barely literate and our perfect offspring are, in fact, spawn from Hell.

We join the PTA. We create a "homework space." We yell a lot. Pretty soon, the terrible truth sets in: We are becoming our parents, and our children are becoming us. "Why do I have to study about stupid plants when I'm going to be a sports commentator when I grow up?" my 9-year-old asks in disgust. His fourth-grade class has 19 boys and 7 girls. It's *The Lord of the Flies* with recess. His teacher is either a saint or heavily medicated. Frankly, I don't really want to know.

Which is why we here at *Wait Wait* are so thrilled to discover how our teachers and our children are finding new, innovative ways to get a big, red F in Life. Celebrity scholars! Scholarships for stoners! Textbooks with more mistakes than Florida's 2000 election count!

Read on—if you can read! If not, don't feel bad about it! Ignorance is no excuse for not knowing! As Dan Quayle said, "What a waste it is to lose one's mind, or not to have a mind is very wasteful. How true that is." Pop quiz on Tuesday.

Why Johnny Can't Read but Feels Really, Really Good about Himself Anyway

Bluff News Story 1) Even if you've left school, or never went, it's not too late to jump on the seminar bandwagon. Here are three stories about seminars for which you can receive credit. Only one is real. It's up to you to guess the real one.

A) Just when you thought the New Age was old news comes the common-wealth of Kentucky with Aura Buffing. The Kentucky Department of Mental Health approved a $50,000 grant to Fountain Life Associates of Louisville, a firm specializing in "sharpening and shining the energy field of the indi-vidual." The company trains people to see their own auras in their mind's eye and to focus it. Particularly adept students claim to be able to see the aura change colors as it becomes more distinct. Fountain Life applied for the grant in order to bring the technique to poor and rural sections of Kentucky.

B) The Canadian branch of furniture giant IKEA became aware that its impeccably laid out stores with floor after floor of perfectly appointed bedrooms and kitchens are the scenes for spats between shopping cou-ples. After reviewing results of a survey, IKEA offered in-store relation-ship seminars for its customers on Valentine's Day, helping couples shop together peacefully. "We don't want people to fight at IKEA," said spokeswoman Christina Beasley. Susie O'Brien, a professor of pop cul-ture at Canada's McMaster University, pinpoints the danger thusly. "You get an overload of that domestic perfection. You're there on a Saturday morning with your crying 4-year-old who's asking for a meatball. It makes you feel defeated." Apparently, the seminars were well attended.

C) The Massachusetts Turnpike Authority held an "Imagineering" Seminar with its tollbooth collectors to devise ways of controlling the road rage of Turnpike tollbooth patrons. Tim O'Sullivan, toll vendor at the 15A exit at Riverside, came up with a version of an old teenage prank: Offer each cus-tomer the chance to pay for the vehicle in back of them. Usually, the mo-torist will do it, but when the occasional Scrooge balks, the Authority picks up the tab, banking on the notion that not many will want to break the chain of goodwill. "Our customers are loving it," says O'Sullivan, "They laugh their butts off when I tell them and then I see them drive off, looking to thank the other driver instead of chasing them down to flip them off."

Who Said This?   **2) "A thorough appreciation of literature allows no shortcuts."**

Answers on Pg. 126

Fill in the Blank 3) A school in Germany was carrying out some repairs when they discovered a hidden trove of _____ dating from the 1970s.

Pick One 4) Many of those slugabed college students who sleep through their morning classes are the beneficiaries of scholarships awarded because of financial need or a 40-inch vertical leap. Buck Wolf of abcnews.com dug up information about scholarships aimed at students with more unusual qualifications. One scholarship involves illegality. Is it:

A) The NASCAR scholarship for the removal of speed limits

B) The pot scholarship

C) The John Gotti scholarship

5) Some scholarships are designed to attract or reward particular scholars, such as the Gertrude J. Deppen scholarship at Bucknell College in Pennsylvania. What are Deppen scholars rewarded for?

A) Not smoking, drinking, taking drugs, or participating in "strenuous athletic contests"

B) Mastering the ancient but underappreciated musical instrument: the Jew's harp

C) Getting into Bucknell with the lowest high school grade-point average of any entering freshman

Answers on Pg. 126

Bluff News Story 6) **Here are three stories of school drama in the news. One is real, but the other two get an F in the truth department. It's up to you to guess the real one.**

A) It's the Revenge of the Lunch Ladies in Frederick, Wisconsin. Two cafeteria workers at the Mordecai Brown Middle School were arrested for forcibly detaining a sixth grader who had thrown several meatballs at them while shouting that he "wouldn't even feed you this food!" The two women grabbed the boy and tied him to a metal rack while encouraging the boy's classmates to throw their meatballs at him, which precipitated a general food fight in which a teacher was injured by an airborne bowl of pudding. The boy's parents filed a complaint and the two cafeteria workers were hauled away in handcuffs the next day.

B) The U. S. Supreme Court will consider whether the practice of paper swapping—kids passing test papers among their seatmates to be graded—violates students' privacy rights. The Tenth U. S. Circuit Court of Appeals in Denver ruled that the practice violated the Federal Family Education Rights and Privacy Act, which keeps students' records confidential. Some parents and teachers feel the students aren't responsible for grading and that teachers should do their own work, no matter how convenient the system is. But Maureen Ponterelli, a sixth-grade teacher in Rhode Island, says that she's fighting the perception that teachers who paper swap go home in the evenings, and "watch the soap operas, sit on the couch eating bonbons with their feet up."

C) A school district in Chino, California, had to pay damages when two children with peanut allergies fell ill after they swapped sandwiches with other kids at lunch. As part of the settlement, the schools agreed to maintain lists of every student's allergies, to remove any possible allergy-triggering items from vending machines at school, and to hire a medically trained cafeteria monitor to inspect the lunches the children bring from home and make sure they're not trading food. Leonard Tunnel, the district superintendent says, "It's just cheaper for us to add a full-time staff person to monitor this than it is to keep going to court with these lawsuits. That could wipe us out."

Pick One

7) The Zolp Scholarship, offered by Loyola University in Chicago, offers 4 years of full tuition to a qualified student who:

A) Is named "Zolp"

B) Is willing to work as valet to the school's president

C) Can speak demotic Greek

 Limerick

8) The headmaster explains, smugly shrugging,
His new measure the PTA's plugging.
"There are no reprimands
For just shaking hands.
But be careful if you get caught _____.

9) I am just a political rookie.
But I had good odds, ask any bookie.
I'm suspended, although
I did not offer dough,
But just promised my voters a _____.

10) Since the kids and the teachers drool bunches
This reviewer has chased their cruel hunches
Wolfgang Puck is inferior
To this great cafeteria
They're serving up gourmet _____.

Answers on Pg. 127

Entertainment

intro by
Adam
Felber

The great Peter Ustinov once said, "The young need old men. They need men who are not ashamed of their age, nor pathetic imitations of themselves."

What a blowhard! Today's entertainers know that their function is simply to provide grist for the mill of idolatry or ridicule—not to provide searing sociological insights. If every celebrity had the poise and self-aware sagacity of Ustinov, there probably wouldn't be a *Wait Wait*!

Fortunately for those of us in the business of ridicule, Ustinov was a rare bird indeed. Whatever "the young" may need, we need people who are pathetic imitations of themselves. And thankfully, we get them with reassuring frequency.

Referencing the latest vagaries of the likes of Britney Spears, the WWF, and Sean "Puff Daddy/P. Diddy" Combs would not have been possible on NPR a few short decades ago. But that was before the worlds of high art, low entertainment, and real news had merged together into one glorious, tasteless muddle. Today, with Letterman as an obligatory whistle-stop for serious political candidates, with presidents appearing on MTV, and professional wrestlers governing large states, with actors, pop stars, writers, and politicians apparently unable to tell the difference between one and the other like a population of over-achieving Sneetches, we have truly entered a beautiful, valueless age.

We at *Wait Wait* applaud the applause-seekers, for their quest is our food. Of course, the paradox here is we ourselves are technically entertainers. If you were to go backstage before a live *Wait Wait* taping and see Carl's requisite bowl of blue M&M's, Peter's contractual henna bath, or my own fawning entourage, you would see that we fit right in.

The Outer Reaches of Narcissism

Pick One 1) *I Love Lucy* was groundbreaking in many ways. The ad agency for the original sponsor, the Philip Morris Company, was afraid the show might go too far. What were the producers contractually forbidden to do?

A) Change Lucy's hair color from its trademark bright red, even though the show was filmed in black and white

Answers on Pg. 128

B) Feature any character turning down the offer of a cigarette—for any reason

C) Allow Desi Arnaz, a real-life singer and bandleader, to sing unless absolutely essential to the plot

2) One of the ways in which the show did break ground was depicting Lucy pregnant at a time when you couldn't even say the word "pregnant" on television. How did the producers reassure network and advertising executives that no one would be offended?

A) They promised to have each script approved by a priest, a rabbi, and a minister.

B) At no point would anyone, including Lucille Ball herself, touch her abdomen.

C) When at all possible, Lucy would be filmed either from the back or from the chest up.

3) "When I die I would like to be born again as me."

4) "For the amount of talent I had, I enjoyed a tremendous career."

5) The first _____ seen on TV was on the show *Leave it to Beaver*.

6) To get viewers to tune in to a morning news show, NBC hired _____ as a co-host.

Pick One   7) Fifty years ago, Generoso Pope Jr., armed with a dream and a few hundred thousand dollars in illicit loans from the Mafia, founded the nation's leading supermarket tabloid, the *National Enquirer*. The *Enquirer* began life as a straightforward yet downmarket newspaper in the early 1950s. What inspired Pope to transform the paper into a scandal sheet?

A) The day in 1955 when two dozen people said to Mr. Pope, "Hey, did you hear Marilyn Monroe married Joe DiMaggio?"

B) The day he drove past a traffic accident and noticed all the people staring at it

C) The day his dog coughed up something that looked freakishly like Bob Hope's profile

8) In 1979, Pope launched the *Weekly World News* as a companion to the *Enquirer*. What prompted the new venture?

A) One of the *Enquirer's* psychics told him that the words "weekly," "world," and "news" would result in great fortune.

B) There were some black-and-white presses sitting around unused after the *Enquirer* went to color.

C) Pope made a bet with a friend that he could succeed with a new magazine even more stupid and mindless than the *Enquirer*.

Bluff News Story   9) One of the members of the 1970s rock group the Doobie Brothers has made a name for himself, and not on the *Billboard* charts. Here are three stories of a former Doobie Brother's surprising new project. One is real, but the other two are contrived only to make the producers of *Behind the Music* think they missed something. It's up to you to guess the real one.

A) Former Doobie Brothers bassist, Tiran Porter, has joined the lawsuit filed by the descendents of Sally Hemmings, the slave with whom Thomas Jefferson is said to have conceived several children. Recent DNA evidence has buttressed the claims of Hemmings' descendants and Porter is the great-grandnephew of Walter Hemmings, Sally's grandson, who was himself a cornet player in a Los Angeles marching band. "I always heard from the old folks in my family that we had some connection with Jefferson," Porter said. "Now it seems like the long train has finally run to me." Porter plans to request that he one day be buried in the Jefferson-Randolph family plot at Monticello.

B) If you examine some of the Doobie Brothers' late '70s albums, including their 1976 double album *Doobie Brothers Live*, you might notice the oddly familiar name of a young backup keyboardist, Corey Flint. Now, as some of National Public Radio's more obsessive fans have learned over the years, this is indeed none other than NPR's afternoon newsman, Corey Flintoff. Flintoff, then 19, got the job filling out the Doobie sound in 1975 and for $2\frac{1}{2}$ years, he played mainly Hammond organs and synthesizers behind Michael McDonald's piano work. His earlier incarnation became news again last week when Flintoff accepted an invitation to play a handful of shows in a Doobie Brothers reunion tour this summer. "I wasn't surprised they were listeners," says Flintoff. "They were always bright, curious guys. But I was kind of shocked that they remembered me."

C) According to an Air Force spokesman, former Doobie Brothers guitarist Jeff "Skunk" Baxter has become "a very knowledgeable advisor to the Pentagon on high-level security issues." Baxter, 52, recently told the *Washington Post* that he gave a paper he had written to his friend, Republican California congressman Dana Rorbacher. Soon, he found himself at the Pentagon with the members of the Ballistic Missile Defense Organization. Baxter says that he really enjoys "the doctrine and the theology" of the work. "I deal with pretty much everything from the nature of the threat to the technologies and the BMCC, Battle Management Command and Control, to acquire, track, identify, and create a firing solution to defeat that threat," he explains.

Answers on Pg. 129

Pick One   10) MIT Press has released *Supercade*, a visual history of the golden age of video games. According to *Supercade*, the very first video game—something called Tennis for Two—was invented for what purpose?

A) To allow two morbidly obese computer programmers to play a non-physically taxing game

B) To assuage the fear of RCA executives that people would get bored with available TV programs

C) To assuage the public's fears of nuclear weapons labs

11) Space Invaders, of course, was the first video game phenomenon. It was so popular that it directly caused what crisis soon after its debut in 1978?

A) The physics department of University of California at Berkeley had to reschedule their spring final exams because 70 percent of the Space Invaders–crazed students failed them

B) A crippling shortage of yen coins in Japan, as they were all being pumped into the arcade game

C) The first epidemic of carpal tunnel syndrome

12) Not surprisingly, many magazines ban words not because they're outlandish but because they're too predictable. Which of these is a real magazine's editorial policy?

A) *Town and Country* magazine bans the word "rich" from its pages.

B) The men's magazine *Maxim* does not allow its contributors to use the word "babe."

C) *Vanity Fair* does not allow the diminutive "starlet" to be used.

Answers on Pgs. 129–130

13) "I never get the girl. I wind up with a country instead."

14) "She never meant that it necessarily applied to her."

15) The University of Iowa marching band has been told not to sing _____ anymore because the lyrics send the "wrong message" about drinking.

16) A performer in San Francisco will be staging his new one-man play in a rented, genuine _____.

17) Undergraduates at Britain's Cambridge University were shocked when instead of having to analyze Shakespeare and Keats in their English finals, they were asked to discuss the works of _____.

18) Philadelphia gallery curator Nick Cassaway's novel idea for an art show went horribly awry because the gallery asked people to _____ the art.

Limerick

19) As a smart, tough, and dangerous tease
I had lines like, "Fork over two g's."
I began as a vamp
And then moved on to camp,
So they called me the Queen of the _____.

Pick One **20) At the *New Yorker*, some editors once managed to concentrate all the words—other than obscenities—banned by the famous former editor William Shawn into one sentence. What was that sentence?**

A) Irregardless of the quid pro quo, the forward-looking idea man suffered no fools gladly, and wasn't timorous about impacting the bottom line.

B) Intrigued by the massive smarts of the bright, balding, feisty, prestigious workaholic, Tom Wolfe promptly spat on the quality photo located above the urinal.

C) Gadzooks! The groovy movie mogul wargamed his high concept until the wise men were in a lather of hip, bigtime stroking.

21) Music acts are famous for their demands, which are usually listed in what is called a contract rider and is part of their legal agreement to perform. We were a little surprised to see some of the things on Britney Spears' list. What did she demand?

A) A fully functional harpsichord, so she can relax by playing Bach

B) A full-size poster of Mickey Mouse to remind her of her Mickey Mouse Club days

C) A box of Captain Crunch, a box of Fruit Loops, and two boxes of Pop Tarts

22) Shania Twain, the diminutive country pop star with the killer abs, demands what in her dressing room?

A) An entire convenience store–type plastic tub of Slim Jim brand beef jerky

Answers on Pgs. 131–132

B) Some cardboard boxes, so that she and the band can take the left-overs with them

C) Seventy gallons of whole milk for bathing

23) Designer Manolo Blahnik has withdrawn a new pair of _____ from the market, saying they might be used as a weapon.

24) A California company is offering celebrities the opportunity to copyright their _____.

25) According to the BBC, reactions ranging from amusement to horror have greeted an electronic jacket which inventors say helps train budding _____.

26) Actor David Soul won a libel case against a critic who said a play that the former Hutch from *Starsky and Hutch* starred in was the worst he'd ever seen. It wasn't the bad review that won the case, it was the fact that the critic had _____.

27) "I bet you wish I was a puppet so you could stick your hand up my [rear] and make me do what you want!"

Pick One

28) What specific requirement does the band the Wallflowers demand of its promoters?

A) Never refer to leader Jakob Dylan, Bob Dylan's son, as "Bob Dylan's son"

B) That no beverage in the arena be sold in Styrofoam or other nonrecyclable containers

C) That members of the crew refrain from approaching, talking to, or even looking at the band starting 2 hours before the show

29) Roger Richman of Beverly Hills, California, is a sort of lawyer to the dead stars. Among Mr. Richman's clients are the Wright Brothers. For the centenary of their flight at Kitty Hawk, Mr. Richman licensed a number of commemorative products, including which of these?

A) The Wright Brothers' signature Learjet for 12 million dollars

B) An $18,000 platinum pen with a bit of fabric from the actual airplane encased in it

C) The complete Wright Brothers' flight suit ensemble, complete with knickers and vulcanized goggles

30) One of the reasons Mr. Richman more or less invented the business of dead-celeb licensing is that celebrity images were so terribly exploited. Which of these is an actual item in his personal collection of unauthorized horrors?

A) Dr. Freud's Pillow Talk, a pillow that analyzes you when you pull a string

B) The Joan Crawford coat hanger

C) The Isadora Duncan extra-long driving scarf

Answers on Pgs. 132–133

31) "Ba-flump-bump-a-dump-ump"—oh, bummer.
This solo could last the whole summer.
Despite difference in style
I'll shut up and smile
For fear we might lose our last _____.

32) In a recent poll, film critics voted *Some Like It Hot* the funniest movie of all time, while the American public chose _____.

33) At a recent Miss Universe pageant, Miss Israel wore a stunning gem-studded vest over her gown, made of _____.

34) In 1977, there were 150. Now there are 85,000. If that growth rate continues unchecked, in 20 years, one-third of the world's population will be _____.

35) Some Canadian pediatricians are warning parents about a group of suspicious characters in the children's story _____ who are obsessive-compulsive, chronically depressed, under-medicated and gender-confused.

36) "I put the dolls, to be succinct, in compromising positions with kitchen appliances."

37) "It is the most successful journalistic scam I have seen in my entire adult lifetime. A catastrophic fraud. Corrupt, intellectually bankrupt, and revolting."

Pick One 38) We of the GI Joe generation remember GI Joe's distinguishing characteristic: a scar on his cheek. Why did every GI Joe have that scar?

A) To show that he was not merely a company clerk or back-of-the-lines loafer, but a true masculine man of action

B) Because the first mold had a flaw which wasn't discovered until they had made thousands of heads, so they called it a scar

C) As an intentional distinguishing characteristic, to foil counterfeiters

39) GI Joe was first presented at the 1964 Toy Fair with great fanfare and a press package that contained at least one egregious lie.

A) That GI Joe's face was modeled from a composite of 20 actual Medal of Honor winners

B) That a poll of 10,000 young boys showed they admired the American fighting man more than Batman, Superman, or Mickey Mantle

C) That future GI Joe accessories would include a working submarine, a firing machine gun, and an aircraft carrier

Bluff News Story 40) Aside from their well-loved halls of old master paintings and cases full of dried bugs, museums are trying to be innovative. Here are three stories of museums forced to return to the drawing board. One exhibit is real, but the other two were curated only for you. It's up to you to guess the real one.

A) The Museum of Natural History in London was planning the dinosaur exhibit to end all dinosaur exhibits: a model of a Tyrannosaurus Rex complete with foul, rotten meat–scented breath

Answers on Pg. 134

that would waft through the exhibit via electric scent diffusers. But the museum scaled back their aspirations after consulting with Dale Air De-odorizing, the company they contracted to make the smell. In the end, the curators chose the acrid, earthy smell of the T-Rex's boggy environment instead of the T-Rex itself, described by one paleontologist as "the most putrid, foulest thing that ever lived."

B) Hoping to improve police/community relations after a series of highly publicized wrongful arrest suits, the Beverly Hills Police Department called in an image consultant who suggested "Good Cop, Bad Cop: Shades or Shady?", a free exhibit for schoolchildren at the department's soon-to-open two-room museum.

C) Officials in Budapest announced that they have cancelled plans to build the International Museum of Plagues in that city. Two years ago, a worldwide medical consortium began planning a center for historical re-search into the role that the bubonic and other plagues have played in world history. The staff of the museum already had begun gathering ar-tifacts and planning exhibits, including a crown that was worn by the ac-tual King Wenceslas, whose prayerful intercession on behalf of plague victims in 1579 gave him his first fame.

Fill in the Blank

41) TV viewers worldwide mourned the decision to cancel *Baywatch*, **but** _____ **are especially upset over the end of the ultimate in jiggly televised entertainment.**

42) Talk about an economic recession has artists in the _____ **industry rubbing their hands in anticipation.**

43) More than 20 years ago, a man named Glenn Hughes answered an ad that said "Seeking gay singers and dancers. Very good-looking and with moustaches," which wound up resulting in his stardom in _____ **.**

44) A study released by the Institute of Psychoanalytic Psychiatry in Rome states that out of 2,000 participants, one-fifth reported that they had a "fleeting but intense erotic encounter with a stranger" after looking at _____.

45) An art opening in London by controversial artist Damien Hirst was cut short when someone _____.

46) A clown in Walnut Creek, California, says he won't stop _____ in his act, even though he's been expelled from a local festival.

Pick One   **47)** Wonder Woman was invented in 1941 by William Moulton Marston, a Harvard-trained psychologist. He said at the time that he saw a need in comic books for what?

A) A patriotic woman who would inspire wartime housewives

B) A strong, powerful woman who could fulfill the desire of male comic book readers to be dominated

C) A way to teach the classical virtues of bodily and mental purity to young men in a way they would find appealing

48) Dr. Marston's other claim to fame was his invention of the systolic blood pressure gauge, which led directly to the first lie detector, which operated much like Wonder Woman's golden lasso. According to the *Washington Post*, how did he test his prototype device?

A) He attached it to his own arm, and took readings while he called up random numbers and pretended to be "Willemina Mars."

Answers on Pgs. 135–136

B) He would use it on his teenage children every morning to quiz them about their activities the night before.

C) He hired sorority girls to wrestle each other while wearing the device.

49) Eva, Zsa Zsa, and the Zeppo Marx–like Magda Gabor—the Hungarian glamour pusses may who may be the first people in history to be famous for being famous—were known for their romantic lives. Who, according to Zsa Zsa, was her first lover?

A) Swashbuckling movie star Douglas Fairbanks

B) Kemal Attaturk, founder of modern Turkey

C) Noted physicist Enrico Fermi

50) "I probably would have married a conservative banker, played golf, and become an alcoholic."

51) "Take away the pop-eyes, the cigarette, and those funny clipped words and what have you got? She's phony, but I guess the public likes that."

52) "She was multi-talented from the start, but with the social instincts of a landlady. [She's] only interested in [herself], and her only marriage that will survive is the one between her ego and her career."

53) "I wouldn't even think about playing music if I was born in these times. I wouldn't even listen to the radio."

Pick One 54) Eva Gabor—the *Green Acres* star—once got into an elevator with a handsome plastic surgeon from Beverly Hills. She batted her eyes and said, "Do I know you?" How did the man respond?

A) "We've never met, but I have a design patent on your nose."

B) "Not yet, but we've got 17 floors to go."

C) "Yes, I was your third husband."

55) Pick the attraction that commemorates a part of history we didn't think anybody wanted to remember.

A) Stalin World, a theme park recreating the depredations of Soviet tyranny in Lithuania

B) Hooverville, a collection of recreated corrugated tin shacks complete with re-enactors playing victims of the Great Depression

C) The Irish Potato Famine Museum, which pointedly offers no potato dishes in the cafeteria

Answers on Pg. 137

Foreign News

intro by
Sue Ellicott

There's always room in our hearts and space on our show to make fun of Sue and her birth people. Oops. Sorry. That wasn't me. I was misquoted, taken out of contest. I mean context. Help. Where are George W. Bush's tutors when you need them? What I meant to say was we're a cosmopolitan bunch here at *Wait, Wait, Don't Tell Me*, thanks to Peter and his childhood in New Jersey, Carl's irresistible Southern charm, and my undying love for Marmite. And we worry that the American people are not getting a fair and accurate picture of the world. So it's the professional broadcaster in all of us, really, that drives us to dredge up details absurd and implausible from goings-on outside the United States. Let's be honest, there are important things out there that Ted Koppel isn't telling. Have you ever heard a BBC

49

World Service newsflash on a talking bus stop in Britain or heard the latest about Moammar Gadhafi's new aviator sunglasses? 'Course you haven't. We go beneath the surface of the news and give you what really counts. Think of us as a benevolent and wittier opposite of those offensive T-shirts that somebody always had in high school. You know, those with the slogan about joining the Army to "travel to exotic places, meet interesting people, and shoot them." Well, forget the khakis. Tune in to us and you'll go nowhere, meet nobody, and get a chance to laugh at everybody everywhere. Amazing, isn't it? And you know the best part? They'll never even know.

Global Warning

Pick One **1) One of the trademark professions of old London has gone away—Bernard Reyner agreed to retire as the last known practitioner of what position?**

A) Seller of pigeon food in Trafalgar Square

B) Top-hatted "Chim-Chiminey Cheroo" chimney sweep

C) Lord High Executioner

Fill in the Blank **2) Pilots on a Scottish flight ruled that more than one hundred passengers were too _____ to fly.**

3) A wealthy Romanian businessman paid $3.5 million dollars for a luxurious home that's part of a compound in Bucharest. It's centrally located with excellent security, but the happy homeowner was surprised when he tried to move into his new home to find that it was _____.

4) Parents at an Australian primary school have decided _____ will help them raise money for their kids.

5) A man in England has been granted a divorce from his wife of 38 years because she wouldn't stop _____.

6) A group of Hong Kong women refused to leave a burning office tower until their _____ were finished.

Limerick

7) Though we think that this promo is rad
   When you look, you might think you've been had.
   It's too tiny to see,
   Wrapped around that bee's knee.
   We've created the world's smallest _____.

8) We Ukrainian wonkas work hard
   To earn the pig lovers' regard.
   We meld chocolate confection
   With porcine perfection.
   Our candy bar's soft core is _____.

Answers on Pgs. 138–139

Fill in the Blank 9) According to the BBC, more Australian companies are giving Christmas bonuses in the form of all-expense paid trips to _____.

10) A store clerk in Berlin thwarted an armed robbery when he repulsed the invaders with _____.

11) The military leaders of Venezuela are extremely upset because somebody mailed them _____ as an insult.

12) A British magazine blamed declining sales of candy to children on the increasing popularity of _____.

13) A German man failed horribly when he tried to warm his car up by _____.

14) Four trains in Japan had to stop while workers searched for a _____.

15) A judge in England accepted a transsexual's excuse that he/she couldn't ride a scooter with a helmet on because _____.

16) A train bound for Surrey, England, was forced to book taxis for its passengers because the engineer _____.

17) British soccer team Oxford United hopes it'll win more games now that its new stadium isn't _____.

Answers on Pgs. 139–141

18) A Polish man avoided paying his $2 cab fare by _____.

19) A _____ was arrested in Burundi after being captured by villagers on suspicion of spying.

20) The French Army is using camouflaged _____ to recruit potential soldiers at movie theaters.

21) In a German hospital, a 95-year old hip-replacement surgery patient said he wouldn't leave until he was assured he could _____.

Limerick

22) You, Highland spy, masked your speech well,
But cabbage and eggs always tell.
Although you kept quiet
Without fruit in your diet
I know you're a Scot by your _____.

23) The sister peeked out from her wimple,
"Come on, this procedure is simple.
Our patient's complexion
Is far from perfection.
Stand watch while I pop this ripe _____."

24) Oh, girlfriend, let's do this again.
Things really picked up after 10.
This monosexed curfew
Has increased our purview.
I'm loving this night without _____.

Fill in the Blank

25) In Britain, half of the people polled said they'd rather give up a year of life than _____.

26) A Scottish man expecting to pick up pictures from his vacation in Greece was instead given pictures of _____.

27) Prince Charles received a visit from 40 women dressed in _____.

28) The _____ association in Britain is changing its name because the moniker is too pedestrian.

29) Villagers are upset over their lost signpost in the Scottish village of _____.

30) A Montreal court ruled that being _____ is not a sign of mental incompetence.

Bluff News Story

31) Every family has one—a member, usually an uncle or aunt, who shows up in the family portraits somewhere off to the side and is spoken of only in hushed tones. Our panelists have three stories about families and their black sheep. One is a real relative in the closet; the other two are not. Your job is to pick the real one.

A) The private lives of the Japanese Emperor and royal family keep leaking out to the public. A book written by esteemed Tokyo University historian Yigato Meriyaki puts a new twist to an old imperial mystery. The book contends that Prince Mikasa Takahito, the youngest brother of Emperor Hirohito, was seldom seen in public because he was a transvestite who amused himself by passing as a geisha, complete with

Answers on Pgs. 142–143

makeup and kimono. This horrified both the Emperor and top Japanese generals, who ordered Japanese spies to "date" Takahito to keep him out of the enemy's sight during World War II. After the war, the prince retired to a monastery in Kyoto, where Professor Meriyaki found elderly monks who fondly remembered the man who insisted on being called Princess Mika.

B) There will probably never be a holiday, a major motion picture, or even a TV movie celebrating the voyages of Frederico Columbus. Although he was, like his celebrated older brother, a sea captain, the younger Columbus' ambitions were more modest. He carried freight from major port to major port and only ventured beyond the Mediterranean Sea four times in his career. But Frederico took full advantage of his brother's name, charging what some considered exorbitant fees for his less-than-groundbreaking voyages. His career ended in 1512 when his ship, the *Santa Katarina*, went down in a storm just 10 miles out of port. Though cleared of any wrongdoing, the stain on his reputation caused him to live out the rest of his life in Venice, where he was known for his lavish parties and dissolute lifestyle until his death in 1521.

C) We know of Charles Darwin's contributions to science, but how about those of his cousin, Francis Galton? Galton came up with the idea of identifying criminals by their fingerprints, but he was also obsessed with the idea of genetic superiority. He coined the term *eugenics* and produced a "beauty map" of Great Britain. With a brass counting device of his own invention hidden in the palm of his hand, he graded the women of each town on a scale of one to five. London, the prettiest—the ugliest, Aberdeen. Galton produced several other studies: pedigree moths, three generations of lunatic cats, and arithmetic by smell.

Limerick   **32) Finland: Think of trees and soft breezes,**
Not seizures or wheezes and sneezes.
Genetic disorders
Exist past our borders.
We're finished with Finnish _____.

33) Though I fear things appear quite austere
Mere job cuts won't shear my career.
Been laid off by Guinness
Don't send violinists,
Just give me my severance in _____.

34) The Japanese monster's a killa.
He'll make you strong like a gorilla.
Hey, kids! Come on, try it.
A reptilic diet.
Just eat this canned meat of _____.

35) No play at work is disconcerting.
It's an issue we're all miniskirting.
Being formal's a fetish.
Come on, be coquettish.
It's time for some on the job _____.

Fill in the Blank

36) A worker at a Jaguar factory in England admitted to stashing pornography inside a car made for _____.

37) Jail officials in Corsica released three prisoners because a _____ had instructed them to.

38) A nursery in Canada had to recall poisonous plants that were labeled _____.

39) A team of Swedish scientists looking for the Loch Ness Monster has been distracted by a man _____.

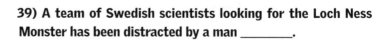

Answers on Pgs. 143–145

40) An outspoken Japanese legislator said that disgraced politicians should be _____.

41) A British policeman being tried on charges of indecent exposure blamed his _____.

42) When confronted by Colombia customs authorities, a family claimed that the $1 million in their bag was given to them by _____.

43) Islamics in Kuwait say a proposed _____ would "bring the wrath of God" down on the country.

44) A man in Aachen, Germany, walked into a brothel and an argument ensued when he ran into _____.

45) German citizens are attempting to change a law requiring them to pass a written test before being allowed to _____.

46) Prince Philip criticized Buckingham Palace for releasing pictures of his grandson Prince William on a trip to Chile because the photos made the Prince look _____.

Who Said This? 47) "This is no constitutionally governed state, this is a land of rhinos! This is legalized robbery by police. I'm surprised they're not authorized to shoot you, too. But of course if they shoot you, they cannot get any money out of you."

Fill in the Blank

48) During World War II, British secret agents carried _____ as a secret weapon. It wasn't lethal, but it was meant to disrupt enemy personnel.

49) A quick-thinking woman in Japan was able to save her 70-year-old father from choking through the timely use of a _____.

50) Authorities on the Solomon Islands in the Pacific Ocean are worried about an increase in concussions among the populace caused by falling _____.

51) Women at a Bristol, England, bingo hall are battling what they say is a workplace danger by refusing to sit in a chair that they say makes women _____.

52) Canadian artist Jonathan Bowser is upset because _____ used one of his paintings for the cover of a new romance novel without permission.

53) An Israeli woman has circulated a list of 68 colorful and inventive insults, including "swamp fly," "gut ripper," and "blood drinker" that she's heard uttered in _____.

54) Slovakia's clergy are joining together to fight _____, an adversary they liken to "a stranger who enters your home, doesn't introduce himself, touches your children, and wants to take them away."

55) In the Pacific kingdom of Tonga, the government is up in arms over millions of dollars that were embezzled by the kingdom's _____.

56) Mike Madden, an inventor from Crackpot Cottage in England, made news when he tried out his new bird-feeding hat, but didn't count on being attacked by _____.

57) A ballet performance at London's Royal Opera House was interrupted by an exploding _____.

58) Scotland Yard investigated complaints that one of its officers _____ at a crime scene.

Pick One   **59)** The *Wall Street Journal* reported that a traditional art in Japan is dying out because of modernization and competition from abroad. What is this difficult and once-valued occupation?

A) Subway pusher—the white-gloved guys who cram people into subways

B) Chick sexer—people trained in the art of determining the sex of very young chickens

C) Wooden food sculpting—making carved imitation food out of wood for restaurant windows

Limerick   **60)** I swear on my mother, it's true.
Ask the guys from the rescuing crew.
We truly are stuck
From the crash of the truck
That was filled with industrial _____.

61) Psychic research remains on its post.
What haunts us has been diagnosed.
Now we know why they've flown.
Who is on a cell phone?
Please hang up, sir, you're spooking the _____.

Answers on Pgs. 145–148

Politics

intro by
**P. J.
O'Rourke**

When we poke fun at politicians, it's just to show how much we love them—love them for the easy laughs they give us by being total jerks.

Oh, we love them anyway. We love politicians for having careers in politics instead of wreaking havoc in other, more important professions. Politicians, for instance, would be terrible athletes. The right fielder has palsy and memory loss. He's confined to a wheelchair. But we can't bench him, he's an eight-term incumbent.

Politicians would seal the official scorecard, subpoena the umpire after every strike call, and demand a recount of the number of bases. The political type of competition is too tough for sports. Imagine no NCAA basketball playoffs because the Maryland-Duke game was killed in committee. And then—competitive as politics is—politicians have fits of bipartisanship that could result in a Super Bowl with the Patriots and the Rams on the same side, playing against no one.

We're happy that politics keeps politicians off the playing field. But we're even happier that politics keeps politicians out of the house. We don't want politicians in our domestic arrangements.

"Where's Mom?"

"Sorry, your mother had term limits. George W. Bush is your new mom."

And we definitely don't want politicians in the kitchen. The sink/stove conference on The Proposal for Take-Out Act crafts a compromise—twice-fried pizza.

Adventures with
Windbag Politicians

Bluff News Story 1) Not everyone is pleased when their city's department of public works comes up with a bright idea for your tax dollars. Here are three stories about public works improvement projects. One is real, and it's up to you to guess which one.

A) What do you do when your ancient tradition of cow reverence clashes with your new high-speed lifestyle? If you're the town of Nigepoor, India, the solution is simple: the cow lane. The once-rural town 100 miles from Bombay is now home to three companies in India's burgeoning high-tech industry. In order to allow for the increased traffic while honoring the sacred cows who frequent the streets, the town recently tore up a 3-meter-wide strip of pavement on two of its most-trav-eled thoroughfares. The lanes were then seeded with sweet grasses and wildflowers to encourage the bovines to use the lane while traversing the town. According to Mayor Rakish Vadicharia, the plan seems to be working so far. "Since the lanes opened in December, the cows do seem to use them and traffic has eased a bit." However, Vadicharia concedes, intersections are still a problem.

B) The city council in Scottish Junction, Nevada, has voted to amend the legal meaning of the yellow light on civic traffic signals from "caution" to "proceed very fast." Council Member Wendy Caanuo said, "Look, it's gotten to the point where no one is slowing down anyway, so why not just change it?" Petitions from area high schools and posters reading "Mello Yello must go!" were overwhelming the city officials and the motion was passed unan-imously. The immediate downside is that there is less revenue from traffic violations, but as Junction High School senior Sean Lambert says, "This is a new millennium. This is no time to slow down. It's about progress."

C) Just when it seemed like the city of Barcelona, Spain, couldn't get any nicer, now even their trash collection is about to improve. Soon, the Cattle Land capital will be installing microchips in its 18,000 public litter bins to monitor their use. Using handheld computers, Barcelona sanitation workers will be able to read each bin to see how full it is, when it was last emptied, and even maybe if it needs a new coat of paint. Officials hope the wired bins will help to streamline collection routes to keep the busiest bins the cleanest and see the $113,000 cost of the program as money well spent.

2) The EPA is permitting the spraying of caffeine in Hawaii to control a population of _____.

3) California Governor Gray Davis signed a bill that will improve the working conditions of _____.

4) A city councilman in Cape Coral, Florida, has a proposed a ban on thong bikinis because they cause _____.

5) A Maryland Court of Appeals overturned a man's conviction for _____ while intoxicated.

6) An alderman in St. Louis is being criticized because she _____ during a filibuster.

Pick One 7) Merely serving in the highest office in the land does not guarantee you'll be treated with respect once you leave office. President James Buchanan left office under a bit of a cloud, caused by, among other things, the South's secession from the Union. Congress, however, acted to give him tribute where tribute was due. What did Congress do as an expression of gratitude for his service?

A) After the first experimental U. S. Navy submarine sank immediately on its first trial, they retroactively named it the U. S. S. Buchanan.

B) They removed his portrait from the Capitol so it wouldn't be vandalized.

C) They passed a resolution forbidding members from calling him names during Congressional debate.

Who Said This? 8) "The cheek of every American must tingle with shame as he reads the silly, flat and dishwatery utterances of the man who has to be pointed out to intelligent foreigners as the President of the United States."

Answers on Pgs. 149–150

Limerick

9) "Get a grip," the white settler commands.
"You've seen sillier things on your lands.
So we do not have qualms
About rubbing our palms.
What's so funny when we're shaking _____?"

Bluff News Story

10) Every now and again, we check in on what legislators have been doing. Here are three stories about lawmakers at work. One is real, but the others are just whimsy. It's up to you to pick the real one.

A) Rwanda's tiny parliament has enacted an emergency measure banning entry of flightless birds into the central African nation. Problems have arisen with runaway and aggressive ostriches at refugee camps in Rwanda, filled with tens of thousands of escapees fleeing from neighboring Congo. The uncontrollable ostriches have caused several severe human injuries. "We have a big enough catastrophe already," Pascal Nogorgot, Rwanda's ambassador to the African Union, told the BBC. "These weird and greedy birds just have to go."

B) There was a hot time in the Wisconsin legislature when State Representative Larue Shermehorn proposed a bill banning the depiction of the American flag, or any other patriotic symbol, created out of cheese. At a recent reception at the state capitol, a large cheddar carved to look like the President and Mrs. Bush was placed near a heat vent, causing it to melt into a lumpy mass. The *Madison Capital Times* ran before and after photos, and the newspaper was beset with angry calls, letters, and e-mails. "We simply can't run the risk in these times when we must all rally behind our President that he will become a pile of goo on the floor," said Representative Shermehorn, whose bill also forbids the depiction of the U. S. Capitol, the White House, the Washington Monument, the Lincoln Memorial, Vice President Cheney, Mrs. Cheney, and Colin Powell.

Answers on Pg. 150

C) Previous legislation introduced by Dorothy Pelote in the Georgia House of Representatives has failed to pass. For instance, her bill to prohibit the state's students from growing long fingernails and her bill to prohibit the state's supermarket baggers from licking their fingers never won support. Now, Representative Pelote's got another hot-button issue. She will sponsor a bill that prohibits Georgians from answering their doorbells naked. Pelote explains, "The current law allows a person to come to the door naked. It just doesn't let him go outside. I don't even want him coming to the door naked." Pelote's proposal has brought her considerable media attention.

Fill in the Blank

11) The City of San Diego is considering regulations aimed at making its _____ smell better.

12) The *Chicago Tribune* reported that the Web site of Illinois politician Kathleen Thomas featured the phrase _____ in the title at the top of the screen.

Pick One

13) The annual Gridiron Club dinner is a Washington institution that invites the sitting President every year for a dinner in which he is the subject of various jokes presented by the wags of the Washington press corps. Every year, the club has managed to insult the president without ruining anybody's dessert—with one exception. What happened?

A) In 1978, Jimmy Carter walked out in protest over a skit portraying him as a hayseed.

B) In 1907, Teddy Roosevelt got into a shouting match with Senator Joseph "Fire Alarm" Foraker, which made all the diners flee.

C) In 1922, Warren Harding had to cancel his appearance because, it was revealed years later, he was too drunk to speak.

Fill in the Blank

14) The state of Alabama is up in arms over a U. S. government office there that is paid nearly half a million dollars a year to watch _____.

15) According to the *New York Post*, Senators Trent Lott and Strom Thurmond do not allow women staffers to wear _____.

16) The Berkeley, California, City Council decided that to ensure their safety, pedestrians should _____ while crossing the street.

17) Plattsburgh, New York, cancelled the annual holiday house decorating contest because in previous years there were too many _____.

18) The Kentucky Bar Association protested a state highway safety television ad that featured a _____.

19) The Ridgeville, South Carolina, Town Council suspended Mayor Allen Bozardt's pay because they say the mayor has done _____.

20) According to *Family Tree* magazine, as many as 100 million Americans are _____.

Limerick

21) Your German exchange tour just stunk.
You swilled beers and snored in your bunk.
And, oh, Mayor Lueck,
It's "Fuer-sten-feld-bruck"
You'd know that if you weren't so _____.

22) Though I'm 18 and listen to Slayer,
I'm the town's top municipal player.
When I did my report
The town council would snort:
"Just you try it." I did. Now I'm _____.

Pick One

23) The rules of the Gridiron dinner allow for the President to make his own, hopefully humorous remarks at the end of the evening, but sometimes Presidents have been known to appear onstage during the skits. Which of these was an actual Presidential cameo?

A) Richard Nixon and Spiro Agnew in 1970, performing a piano duet

B) Lyndon Johnson, who in 1966, tap danced with his daughter

C) Calvin Coolidge, who in 1923, stood up, glared at the crowd, said nothing, and sat down

Bluff News Story

24) When dealing with the geniuses who shape history, you can't always rely on them to remember every little detail of their lives. Or to report them honestly. Some stories from the lives of the great turn out to be made up, leaving it up to the diligent historian to uncover the true facts. Here are three tales of revised history, one of which is real. The others are fiction based on real events.

A) The ear of Vincent Van Gogh wasn't cut off in a passionate act of self-mutilation, but sliced off by rival artist Paul Gaugin in a fight in 1888. German art historian, Rita Wildegans, after a careful analysis of records and letters, has concluded that Van Gogh and Gaugin got into an alcohol-fueled argument and that Gaugin, the

Answers on Pgs. 151–152

superior swordsman, severed the Dutch artist's ear. Poor Vincent, who suffered from a seizure, could not remember a thing and let Gaugin give the police a detailed account of the incident. Had Gaugin got rid of incriminating evidence? Says Wildegans, "Everything we know about what happened is from Gaugin, but Gaugin was an inveterate liar."

B) The brilliant Charles Dickens is revered as a champion of the poor and downtrodden, especially children, and Dickens spent most of his life burnishing that image. But a new biography by historian Paul Hackman says Dickens was, in fact, more Scrooge than philanthropist. Despite being one of the most successful writers of the 19th century, Dickens was notoriously cheap with servants, tradesmen, and employees, according to unearthed letters and household accounts. After Dickens separated from his wife, Katherine, in 1858, she wrote the courts asking for more support for their ten children. "He'd sooner cut off a finger, than part with a farthing," she complained.

C) It has long been a feel-good fact of American history that at Appomattox in 1865, Robert E. Lee graciously tendered the Confederacy's surrender and Ulysses S. Grant graciously accepted Lee's sole condition—that his soldiers be allowed to keep their horses so they could ride them home for spring plowing. But a letter from Grant to a Mrs. Bixby has surfaced in which he writes, "I was so sick of his holier-than-thou drawl, I made it clear I wanted no more palaver. He then said, 'Can I keep my horse?' I said, 'Hell, no, you'll ride it against us, as soon as our back is turned.'" Lee then threatened to go the newspapers with a certain personal matter about Grant that persuaded him to allow the men to keep their horses.

Fill in the Blank

25) Oklahoma's Department of Human Services was having problems getting people to accept notices of overdue child support payments until they started disguising the documents as _____.

26) According to an investigative report in the *Washington Post*, the Bush White House isn't only unified in pursuit of the President's agenda. The staffers there also seem quite devoted to _____.

27) A British couple was stunned when _____ crashed their wedding reception.

28) In their quest to increase everybody's comfort level, the North Carolina State Senate has passed a bill that forbids people from using profane language while within earshot of _____.

Limerick

29) 'Twas the modus of his operandi
To inter things that might come in handy.
Now a bright South Pole trapper
Discovered a wrapper
It's Admiral Byrd's bar of _____.

Pick One

30) For all its barbed jokes, the Gridiron Club prides itself on being relatively kind—a fact noted by the Dean of White House journalists, David Broder. Broder sums up the evening by saying:

A) "The Gridiron Club dinner sprays the President with ketchup and insists it has drawn blood."

B) "The Gridiron Club dinner is the night of the long butter knives."

C) "What kind of humor can you expect from a club that includes the likes of George Will?"

Answers on Pgs. 152–153

Fill in the Blank   **31)** In Los Angeles, officials are up in arms over a junket by five city employees and two consultants—a fact-finding mission to England and France to inspect _____.

32) In a finding that may confirm an unpleasant stereotype, a political poll found out that Republicans are more likely than Democrats to hand out _____.

33) During the Nixon administration, the White House became concerned that Henry Kissinger might cause an international crisis. To prevent it, instructions were given during State Dinners that Mr. Kissinger was not to be seated near _____.

Bluff News Story   **34)** Some people have managed to take the simple things in life and say, "They're mine!"—leaving the rest of us out in the cold. Here are three stories of people who got there first. One is real, but the other two are still in the public domain. It's up to you to guess the real one.

A) Should old acquaintance be forgot or should they pay royalties? That's the question before a court that is deciding who can sing "Auld Lang Syne" for free. Descendants of 18th-century Scottish poet Robert Burns claim they should be paid whenever the song is performed in public. Scotland's highest court recently ruled that the family should be compensated for the next 50 years when the song is sung in public, and they successfully prevented it from airing during a New Year's Eve bash in London. British judges, of course, reject the suit on the grounds that the folk song has been in the public domain for more than 2 centuries.

B) Still smarting over the spread of Mad Cow disease, the French are now up in arms about the dumping of thousands of liters of

Answers on Pgs. 153–154

Liqueur de Punelle, or Sloe Gin, which is made from a small plumlike fruit that grows in French hedgerows. A glut of sloes after years of short supply has many amateur distillers infusing bottles of gin with the tiny fruit and lining their cellar walls. The results are so good that Paris wine shops have been competing to sell them for up to 400 francs a bottle. But agricultural officials have begun seizing the liqueur, arguing that its sale flouts a law forbidding profits to be made from flora and fauna found on public land. Villagers are so furious they've started to dump their own booty before the feds can get hold of it.

C) When the folks at Albee's Food prepared to package and sell crustless peanut butter sandwiches, they got a stiff warning from a division of Smuckers. It seems that Smuckers had already secured the patent for the "sealed crustless sandwich with peanut butter" and had started selling them as UnCrustables. Patent #6,004,596 from the U. S. Patent and Trademark Office reads, in part, "The sandwich includes a lower bread portion and upper bread portion, an upper filling and a lower filling between the lower and upper bread portions, a center filling sealed between the upper and lower fillings and a crimped edge along the outer perimeter of the bread portions for sealing the fillings there between." Albee's and Smuckers have appealed to the U. S. District Court to resolve the matter.

Pick One **35) Once America became allied with Russia during World War II, the tone of American propaganda toward Communism changed. Which of these is an actual quote from a 1942 *Look* magazine article, "Meet the Real Stalin"?**

A) "He impressed me as quiet and kindly. He is definitely of the 'easy boss' type."

B) "'The children, it's all for the children,' said the generalissimo, bouncing a bright-eyed peasant boy on his knee."

C) "Short in stature, but not lacking in heart, this average Joe is capable of devoting 20 hours a day to his people."

Fill in the Blank

36) Lisle Blackbourn, writing to a Harvard student in the late 1950s, stated, " You have been highly recommended to us . . . as a possible pro prospect." He was writing to _____, who went into another contact sport—politics.

37) The early Congress spent a considerable amount of time considering the fate of the Fredes. The Fredes are _____.

38) New Mexico's Supreme Court has told police in the town of Portales that they have to stop _____ on the traffic tickets they write.

Who Said This?

39) "I have done an in-depth study of drug abuse and Communist brainwashing techniques and I am right in the middle of the whole thing, where I can and will do the most good."

40) "I'm ashamed to say, who is Wheeler?"

Limerick

41) When we fight, it's with great sense of flair.
So I truss up my mane with much care.
I'm not ready for battle
So I've got to skedaddle
Hey, wait, let me finish my _____.

Answers on Pgs. 154–155

Pick One

42) Once the Cold War started for real in the 1950s, it was no holds barred in the propaganda wars. Which of these was used to get our children off to the right start in their ideas of the Commies?

A) Tailgunner Joe's shooting gallery—a toy pellet gun with tin targets representing Russian soldiers

B) The Children's Crusade Against Communism bubble gum cards, with full-color illustrations of Commie leaders, tactics, and principles

C) *The Adventures of Buck Brooks, Menace of the Red Menace*, a Saturday movie serial featuring a teenage anti-Communist crusader

Science

intro by
Roxanne
Roberts

We are embarrassed to report that the *Wait Wait* staff is full of very smart people who know vast amounts of useless information. Need to know the title of a schlocky horror movie from 1967? (Domestic or foreign?) The "B" side of every Herman's Hermits single? (Alphabetical or chronological?) Biker bars that accept American Express cards? (East or West coast?)

But hand us a compass and we can't find North. Ask us to connect the red wire to the yellow . . . oh, dammit! And God forbid we get stranded in space with just a wristwatch (Omega, since you asked) to bring us home. Which is why we love the Professor on *Gilligan's Island* and every other half-baked inventor, mad chemist, and crazy kid with a science fair project and a dream.

They ask questions. Really dumb questions that become even dumber when you really stop and think. Questions about space and time and toasters. Questions about love and money and speed traps. Not to mention waloonphobia and elephant poop. And then they go out and spend gobs of time and other people's money proving that we're all going to die from our cell phones. And that a bird in the hand is worth 2.8834 birds in the bush. Or that people are happier when they have a lot of sex. (Duh.)

Personally, I have always wanted to know why pigeons have red feet. There I was, sitting on a New York park bench thinking great thoughts, and I noticed that all the other city birds have brown feet, but pigeons have red. I pondered this for years, and then I got a life. Which proves my theory: These people have wa-a-a-a-ay too much time on their hands. Which reminds me: Professor, when are you actually going to fix that damn boat?

Blinded by the Pursuit of Knowledge

Bluff News Story 1) If someone builds it, grows it, shrinks it, sets it on fire, or puts it in a small glass enclosure, chances are they will also measure it—to see if it's the biggest, smallest, or most likely to have its own Fox TV special. Here are three tales of measurement. One is real, but the others contain not one grain of measurable truth. It's up to you to pick the real one.

A) The people of Carrickglavin in Ireland have taken to measuring time in increments called Heartland, named after the Heartland Sheepdogs who work the large square meadows outside of town. They now divide their days according to the time it takes the dogs to perform their daily chores. At a quarter Heartland in the morning, the dogs take to the fields and the local greengrocer opens. Full Heartland, they all gather for lunch and the angelus rings in St. Columbus church. And alas, at eleven Heartlands past full, the kennel shuts down and the pub closes.

B) The crunchiness of the pretzels and chips in your pantry may soon be calibrated by a new crunch meter device invented by food scientists in Israel. A sample of food is placed in a small chamber and gradually crushed while microphones pick up the resulting noise and the decibels are plotted into a graph. The resulting ragged line is then converted by a computer into a fractal dimension and then into a number reading. A good crunchy corn flake, for example, gets a reading of about 1.5, says creator Amus Nesenovich. "Once you've established that your potato chip tastes best at a crunch level of 1.4, you can use the crunch meter instead of tasters for quality control," he explained to *New Scientist* magazine.

C) The singles scene in Japan is about to get a whole lot easier if inventor Mariko Obee succeeds in her application for a patent for Love Eyes, a pair of spectacles that can record the dilation of another person's pupils. Behavioral scientists working with animals and humans have known for years that the pupils of a sexually aroused mate increase in size when he or she spies a love interest. Ms. Obee has come up with eyeglasses fitted with a microchip and electrodes that will send tiny pulses from a miniscule camera to a hidden handheld device to alert the wearer with a series of silent pulses if the person doing the looking is turned on. The stronger the pulse, the more powerful the attraction. "Nobody wants to waste time these days picking up wrong signals," she told Tokyo's *Hot Stuff* high-tech magazine.

Limerick

**2) It's scurvy I want to avert
But I do not like fruit for dessert.
Since heat doesn't trouble it,
I'll slip on this doublet.
I get vitamin C from my _____.**

3) The first upright bipedal mammalian
Just might have been Episcopalian
He was Bruce and not Adam
I'm so sorry, madam
Our gene pool's main source is _____.

4) "Who was Galileo's stepdaughter?"
This quiz show is pure mental slaughter.
I just took a sip
Now I feel like a drip
I feel dumb since I've had so much _____.

Pick One 5) Arachibutyrophobia is the irrational fear of

A) Spider-shaped tattoos

B) Saddam Hussein

C) Peanut butter sticking to the roof of your mouth

Bluff News Story 6) Sometimes we're presented with problems that resist solution. We try this, we try that . . . and nada. But then, in our desperation, we draw on our creativity and we find an answer. Here are three stories of necessity mothering invention. One is real, the others are not. Your job is to choose the real tale.

A) Dale Rooks, a Pensacola, Florida, school crossing guard, was frustrated by drivers speeding through his school zone. He tried signaling, waving, yelling; nothing helped. Then Rooks brought a portable hair dryer to work and began pointing it at speeders.

Answers on Pg. 156

Was the hair dryer some kind of radar gun? The drivers hit their brakes. The county school board chairman called the hair dryer one of the most innovative and creative ideas he'd ever seen. Pensacola's Chief of Police was so impressed that he tried the hair dryer himself. Said the Chief, "The first car I pointed it at slowed right down." Of course, there's always the possibility that the drivers aren't fooled. Maybe they're slowing to check their hair in the mirror to see whether they should take advantage of the new grooming service being offered by Pensacola's school system and police force.

B) Gina Nasciemento, a stunning Brazilian daytime TV soap star, planned to dazzle at last week's award ceremony in Rio de Janeiro. But the dress promised to her by the designer Versace arrived two sizes too large. With only hours to go and a second dress failing to show up because of a strike at Rio's airport, Ms. Nasciemento was frantic. She tried tape, a padded brassiere, but no extra cleavage was forthcoming. Eventually, Gina grabbed two of her toddlers' soft toys: a small plush bunny and a baby pink elephant. "I always admired Liz Hurley and her safety pins," Ms. Nasciemento told *Bon Dia* magazine. It worked; at least until she stepped up to the mike to receive a trophy, and the audience heard a little tinkling sound from the bell inside the bunny. Ever the star, Ms. Nasciemento deadpanned into cameras, "My heart is tinkling with happiness."

C) As reported in *Natural History* magazine, Art Ore of Brewster, New York, kept trying to get the bats out of his attic correctly—watching them emerge at dusk to feed on bugs and stopping up the holes before they could come back. But his bats never came out until after dark. Art had one of those mosquito zappers in his yard and he wondered—were the bats lounging around in his attic, waiting for his zapper to alert them when bugs were abundant? To test his theory, Art rigged up a mike and recorded the zapper at night. The next evening at dusk, he played it back. Who-o-om!! Out came the bats! He spotted their hole, stopped it up and the bats had to move on.

Answers on Pg. 157

7) "I have no idea what the first one was. It might have been the first line from Lincoln's Gettysburg Address for all I know. The only thing I know was it was all in upper case."

8) When I say oral hygiene is missing
It's not intimacy that I'm dissing.
In fact, I repeat,
Your lips are so sweet
My teeth could rot from too much _____.

9) When your Sumo frame lands on the mat
And your cartilage goes with a splat
I'll fix your bum knee
With the cause of its plea:
I'll use stem cells derived from your _____.

10) A pain specialist utilizing a spinal cord stimulator to ease chronic back pain has discovered that the device also causes _____.

11) Scientists recently discovered concrete proof of "a mysterious repulsive force, a dark energy, that causes things to break apart and come to an ignominious end." This force is found _____.

Bluff News Story

12) Just when you think two things should not, or could not go together, you read about someone who's combined them for that very reason. Here are three stories of "who'd have thunk it" combinations. One is real, but two are the products of strenuously wishful thinking. It's up to you to guess which is the real one.

A) "Bed and bath" have often been uttered in the same breath, but never before have they occupied the same physical space. Until now, that is. Musaba Shito, Japan's second-largest chain of hotels, announced the opening of its first "shower sleepers" in Kyoto. Guests deposit their belongings in lockers and climb into their dresser drawer–like rooms, set their alarms, and go to sleep. Fifteen minutes before he arises, the sleeper is awakened by a gentle spray of warm soapy water, which gradually increases in intensity. Five minutes later, the room drains and warm air is blown into the berth. The guest emerges clean, dry, and hopefully untraumatized by the experience. Musaba Shito says that so far, response to the shower sleepers is positive and they plan to open three more hotels in Tokyo sometime this year.

B) The Barrelach Candy Company of Unity, Wisconsin, announced that it has invented the world's first candy music box. Each individually wrapped goodie contains a microchip that allows the wrapper to play a song when it is removed. Urban Faber, the president of the candy company, told reporters that the first public sale of the new devices will be targeted at the Christmas rush and that the candies will each play a different Christmas carol. Flavors will include Tannenbaum Crunch, O Come All Ye Coconuts, The First Caramel, and Hark! The Herald Nougat Sings. "We hope soon to have candies and music for all occasions," said Faber.

C) A design undergraduate in England has created a toaster that also forecasts the weather. The futuristic appliance looks and works like an ordinary toaster, but it's actually hooked up to the Internet, where it downloads area forecasts from weather-reporting sites. Twenty seconds before the bread is fully toasted, one of three weather map stencils representing sunny, cloudy, or rainy conditions slides over to mask part of the bread while the rest toasts darker, browning a stencil of the appropriate weather condition onto the slice. The designer, Robin Southgate, said other stencils could print maps or ads or just about any information onto the bread, which should ideally be white (but brown will also work).

13) PEZ candy dispensers first came to the market in 1927. What was the derivation of its unusual name?

A) The German word "pfefferminz," meaning peppermint

B) An ad man's acronym from the phrase "Pills to Encourage Zest"

C) A nonsense word said by the inventor's infant child when first presented with the little candies

14) PEZ is branching out with new products. The first noncandy PEZ product will be:

A) Large, colorful liquid dispensers for home and bar use

B) A CD by the Slackjaws, a group of singing PEZ dispensers, with songs such as "Give Me Some Sugar, Baby" and "You Make Me Look Up"

C) PEZ perfume and bath products

15) Where Sayreville's mud is all slick,
The parasites grow rather thick
This chigger is scary
He's soft and he's hairy.
I've just found the world's oldest _____.

16) Pippi Longstocking's strength makes Evander fall
But her knuckles drag as she meanders, y'all.
She says,"My red hair
Should make you aware
That my ancestor was a _____."

Answers on Pg. 158

17) Geniophobia is the fear of

A) Chins

B) Pleasant people

C) Genies appearing from bottles

18) Waloonphobia is the fear of

A) Ceramic tiles

B) Standing on one foot

C) Walloons, an ethnic group originating in Belgium

Bluff News Story **19) The world is hazardous, but luckily, even as we sleep, people are hatching clever ideas to keep us safe. Here are three stories about new advances in safety. Only one is real. It's up to you to guess which one.**

A) The old days of construction workers whistling at babes may be over. Male chauvinism is a safety hazard, according to a report released by the AFL-CIO. The report claims that 17 percent of all worksite accidents can be traced to "pedestrian distraction." In other words, male workers staring at women. A pilot program in Chicago is testing the random use of tiny surveillance cameras mounted on worker's construction hats, which transmit a video feed to manager's office. The result—less on-the-job ogling and fewer accidents. "Guys will always look at a good-looking woman," says electrician Larry Dellman. "We're just trying to make sure they don't break a leg doing it."

Answers on Pgs. 158–159

B) Falling asleep at the wheel may become impossible thanks to Artificial Passenger software developed at IBM's Watson laboratory. A database of individual driver musical tastes, jokes you like or don't like, and personal history provides Artificial Passenger a full range of provocative gambits such as, "Who was the first person you dated?" and "The stock market went down 500 points—just kidding." If the responses mumbled are incorrect, an alarm may sound, a window is rolled down, or music starts playing. It may also tell you to pull over or suggest you stop at a hotel. The technology will be available in 3 to 5 years.

C) In a recent year, over 15,000 joggers were bitten by dogs badly enough to require medical attention. Hence, the development of Rover Off, a tiny device, which when stepped on emits a squeak too high for humans to hear but just the right pitch to repel dogs. The trouble is, that pitch also attracts owls, giving them the irresistible impression that someone is running along stepping on mice. This year alone, five Rover Off road testers have been mauled in broad daylight by owls. Test joggers are now running in zoos past every kind of caged bird and beast to find the pitch setting that turns dogs away without stimulating any other animal.

Limerick

20) The pilot says, "Bring the hot, wet rag
When things in the plane's kitchenette drag
Flying through time zones
Has whacked out my hormones
My brain has shrunk from too much _____.

21) Guy Ritchie, he gives me the hots.
To score, it won't take many shots.
The Highlands were built
On the freedom of kilts.
The most virile men are the _____.

22) As mothers are apt to remind,
"Your diet and health's intertwined.
If your meals are spectacular
Your ordeals will be macular.
Yes, junk food will make you go _____."

Pick One   **23) Back in the 1950s, in the Golden Age of Tupperware**
parties, the company would encourage women at the party
to play games in order to break the ice. Which of these was a real
Tupperware party game?

A) Shuffle iron, a game in which unplugged electric irons are slid toward targets on a linoleum floor

B) Mystery coffee, a game in which women taste coffee and take turns guessing what common pantry item has been added to the coffee

C) Hubby, a game in which women wrote and then traded classified ads offering to sell their own husbands

Bluff News Story   **24) Here are three stories of dealing with the bleak reali-**
ties of the winter months. One is real, but two are just sea-
sonally affected delusions. It's up to you to guess the real one.

A) Every few years, the city of Buffalo, New York, gets buried under heavy snow, and each year this provides more momentum for the return of the horse-drawn sleigh as public transportation. Tom Drake, the president of the Buffalo Public Sled Association, says that more than 30 of the sleds, which were officially decommissioned in 1939, are still in serviceable condition and would be ideal for occasional use on Buffalo's snowier bus routes. To prove his point, Drake's organiza-

Answers on Pgs. 159–160

tion restored one two-horse sled and ran it, free of charge, along the snow-suspended B15 bus route. The 25-passenger sled carried more than 200 passengers that day.

B) In a plucky display of mind over matter, the town council in Lywin's Daughter, a small town in Finland, voted to eliminate winter by inverting all of the town's calendars. They determined that henceforth in the town, December will be June, January will be July, and February will be August. They have organized summer activities for the children and in a show of good faith, the mayor, Vin Cudahy, swam for 5 minutes in the freezing Lowintin River.

C) The city of Liverpool is looking into a new way to reduce ice and snow on roadways, using elephant dung from the nearby Chester Zoo instead of sand. Complaints that the roadways weren't effectively sanded during winter storms led the city council to consider animal waste, which has already been used successfully on airport runways. A council member did say that a synthetic substance may be used instead, one that like dung is also an effective garden fertilizer.

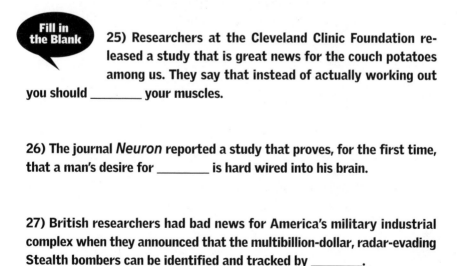

Fill in the Blank

25) Researchers at the Cleveland Clinic Foundation released a study that is great news for the couch potatoes among us. They say that instead of actually working out you should _____ your muscles.

26) The journal *Neuron* reported a study that proves, for the first time, that a man's desire for _____ is hard wired into his brain.

27) British researchers had bad news for America's military industrial complex when they announced that the multibillion-dollar, radar-evading Stealth bombers can be identified and tracked by _____.

Pick One   28) The Tupperware Company depended on its party hostesses for sales and went to some lengths to reward them.
To which of these could a 1950s Tupperware hostess aspire?

A) Having their deepest wish granted by a Tupperware "Wish Fairy"

B) Having their sculptures made in plastic by Tupperware designers

C) A complete replica set of Tupperware Wonder Bowls, rendered in fine
Wedgwood china

Limerick   29) Houston, this is a disgrace.
See the crew's Dionysian embrace?
The ship's called *Apollo*!
But that seems to ring hollow.
They took pregnancy tests out to _____.

30) In your belly's soft fulcrum I squint
At the fluff that is bluish in tint.
Soon my face starts to frown,
"Why is this stuff called down
If it's all upward movement for _____?"

31) The biotechnologist's punchy,
"I'll inject where the stalks get all bunchy.
Some wax in these plants
Will reduce breakfast rants
For your cornflakes will always stay _____."

Answers on Pgs. 160–161

32) "This vintage's a mere 8 months young."
"It's fertilized with chicken dung."
The taste tests are quicker
'Cause it's not a licker.
It's electric: my new handheld _____.

Bluff News Story

33) Here are three stories of fairy tales come true. One is real, but the other two are made up. It's up to you to guess the real one.

A) Researchers in Chicago have discovered what they call the Pinocchio Effect. Turns out that when we lie our nasal tissues actually fill with blood and our nose grows. The expansion is probably caused from a reaction to hormones released when we lie. Noses may not visibly increase in size, but they may get a little red and swollen and even itch, causing liars to touch their noses and reveal their guilty consciences. As part of the study, Dr. Alan Hirsch and colleagues at the Smell and Taste Foundation in Chicago studied the tapes of President Bill Clinton's false Monica Lewinsky testimony and noted that when the President touched his nose more often he was lying.

B) It seems that Prince Charming's habit of kissing slumbering maidens like Snow White and Sleeping Beauty may have been just what the doctor ordered. According to a study conducted at Kinshasa University in the Congo, attacks of a certain variety of sleeping sickness can be cured with simple mouth-to-mouth resuscitation. Sufferers of Somnophelia Neuralgia have underperforming respiratory reflexes while they sleep, resulting in shallow breathing and an inability to wake up. The cure: gentle mouth-to-mouth resuscitation. Dr. Leonard Embasha points out that gentle pressure applied rhythmically to the diaphragm can be just as effective, though aspiring Prince Charmings would probably find that less romantic.

C) A German doctor says every child should eat at least 2 tablespoons of ginger every day and she's basing that recommendation on the famous fairy tale of Hansel and Gretel. Isabelle Stroller, a 32-year-old professor of nutrition at the University of Cologne, says the story of the Wicked Witch in her gingerbread house is based on a real 16th-century Bavarian baker, Hildegard Bouvairen, who fed peasant children from a famine-stricken village a coarse wheat bread loaded with the then-rare and expensive spice, ginger. Stroller recreated the recipe and fed the rustic bread with the spice to undernourished children in local schools and shelters. The results, Stroller reports, were remarkable. The children who ate the gingerbread gained weight, energy, and focus in record time.

34) "It would be a very low tone. Not even whales could hear it."

35) Tupperware has been more than happy to change with the times. Who of these people was the best-selling salesperson in Los Angeles in 1996?

A) Pam Teflon, a drag queen who hosted parties wearing a platinum page boy wig and spangled gloves

B) Darcy Death D'norio, a self-described Goth dominatrix and homemaker

C) Antipholus, an ancient spiritual being channeled by Anne Marie Chisholm, a 52-year-old accountant

Answers on Pg. 161

Stupid Criminals

intro by
Charles P. Pierce

We at *Wait Wait* often give thanks that so many of our more felonious fellow citizens are so bad at their jobs. In part, this is because we all live in lovely homes containing cash, jewels, and many very expensive—and easily fenced—electronic devices. (For a small consideration donated to your local NPR station, you may receive a handsome leather-bound edition of this book's companion volume: *Wait, Wait Stars: Where They Live and What Time They Get Home.*) It is impossible to imagine how we would get a show together every week if somebody, somewhere didn't decide to stick up a Burger King and demand a Whopper at gunpoint.

Look, America always has brought fame and legend upon the successful criminal: Jesse James, John Dillinger, Oliver North. But where is the gratitude of a grateful nation for those who do us law-abiding folks the incalculable service of being both miscreants and dumb as a bag of hammers? Right here, is where. So, go ahead, let them library books pile up into the triple digits. Squeeze the dinner rolls in Philly and mow the lawn naked in Maine. Get busted. You have the right to a single phone call, so call us. We'll make your bail.

Favorite Felonious Citizens

Fill in the Blank 1) An Indiana man was busted for buying cocaine from a policeman who was _____.

2) A Philadelphia man convicted of _____ was sentenced to probation and a $1,000 fine.

3) A man in Wells, Maine, was arrested for driving his car in a _____ while under the influence.

4) A Connecticut robber held up a Burger King and demanded _____.

5) A bank teller in Akron, Ohio, thwarted a robbery when she _____.

Answers on Pgs. 162–164

6) A man in Elmont, New York, was unsuccessful in attempts to rob a gas station brandishing a _____.

7) California police are looking for a repeat bank robber who is being identified by his _____.

8) A Nevada man was convicted of robbing people by pretending to be their _____.

9) A woman pulled over for drunk driving failed to impress the police officer by _____.

10) A South Carolina man was apprehended and arrested for robbing a Food Lion grocery store of _____.

11) Police in Detroit have captured an Alabama man 44 years after he escaped prison where he was serving a term for stealing _____.

12) In California, a hit-and-run driver was turned in by his _____.

13) A California city council candidate spent 5 days in jail for stealing money from a _____.

14) A judge in Georgia convicted a _____ for breaking and entering.

15) A man in Ohio was apprehended by police after he was observed sitting in his car with an "abnormal" amount of _____.

92   wait, wait . . . don't tell me!

16) An Ohio man has been accused of impersonating a highway patrol officer so he could _____.

17) Five masked men who robbed an Athens, Georgia, post office made off with two full sacks of _____.

18) A Minnesota man was arrested at his home by four policemen for possession of _____.

19) A couple in Vermont were arrested after they _____ another person's home without permission.

20) A 60-year-old North Carolina man was arrested after he went to police to report that someone had stolen his _____.

21) A Texas man was caught after years of bilking banks when someone finally became suspicious of his alleged firm, named _____.

22) A man in Ohio who blasted his car stereo too loudly was sentenced to _____.

23) A man in Connecticut was arrested for burning a _____ because he thought it was possessed.

24) A North Carolina resident was found guilty of _____ with his girlfriend.

Answers on Pgs. 164–167

25) Two Ohio men accused of criminal damage to property were given the choice between 60 days in jail or _____.

26) A fugitive from justice in San Diego was apprehended wearing a shirt that read _____.

27) A federal grand jury has indicted a Miami man for allegedly entering the country carrying _____.

28) An armed robbery attempt by a group of armed men failed when the men were _____.

29) A Vancouver woman claimed in court that she couldn't take a Breath-alyzer test because of her _____.

30) A convict in Vermont was caught breaking back into jail after _____.

31) A would-be Finnish robber was captured just 3 minutes after the bank alarm sounded. Police explained the quick capture by saying that the robber forgot to bring a _____.

32) In Florida, two thieves successfully broke into a house and stole two televisions, but were apprehended when they returned to the house. They returned to the house to get the _____.

33) An arsonist in Hamburg, New York, gleefully set fire to a doughnut shop, and then, quite by accident, phoned _____.

34) Ira Monas, age 55, has been charged with running a stock market con game in which he bilked victims out of millions of dollars by convincing them to invest in stocks that he never acquired for them. That's not so strange these days but what's surprising is that Mr. Monas based his business in _____.

35) A bank robber in San Francisco was apprehended after he left his _____ at the scene of one of his crimes.

36) An inmate in a California prison last week managed to successfully jump the fence, only to find himself in _____.

37) A bank robber in Tennessee was caught after his holdup note was discovered in his _____.

38) In Connecticut, a man was convicted of federal weapons charges because he used a _____ as a deadly weapon.

39) A robber was caught in rural Louisiana, despite the fact that he took off all his clothes so that he would be _____.

40) A woman in Orange County, California, was arrested after assaulting another woman with a _____.

41) Four men broke into a veterinarian's office looking to steal the popular painkiller OxyContin, but instead ended up nabbing a drug that _____.

Answers on Pgs. 168–170

42) Edwin V. Gaynor decided that what he wanted to be, more than anything, was a Baltimore police officer. But things went wrong after he answered that he had _____ on the application.

43) A pair of masked robbers in Britain were caught when they forgot to _____.

44) A woman in California attacked the manager of a Ralph's Supermarket with her shopping cart and injured a police officer over _____.

Miscellaneous

intro by Peter Sagal

Two centuries ago, Carl Linnaus created the first classification system that effectively organized man's understanding of the natural world. All living creatures were divided into kingdom, then genera, phylla, families, species ... and then, we presume, just as today, the odd things that were left over were shoved to the back of the book and the Host got forced to write an introduction. I mean, why not? I've pretty much been sitting here, since the beginning of the book, while everybody else did the heavy introducing, and it's about goddamn time I did something to earn those Big Host Dollars. (There's not a lot of them, this being public radio, but they're actually big. About 20 inches by 30. With a big picture of Robert Siegel in the middle.) So ... much as you do when you try to figure out how to take a deduction for the leopard-skin bra and panties you bought for the Christmas office party, we're turning to the Miscellaneous column with a sense of relief. We don't know what these items are, categorically speaking—fish? Fowl? Some horrendous creature from a planet with non-carbon based life? (Does it ever bother you that you're a carbon-based life form? Think charcoal. Think pencil lead. Think you.)

We use a variety of criteria around the *Wait Wait* office to pick stories for our show: some because they're relevant, some because they're an unexpected view into an already well-known event, some because it means Carl gets to do a particularly funny voice. (How much do you think we really care about Britney Spears?) But the one sure way for a story to get into the show is when it makes us laugh. All these stories made us laugh; we don't really know why any more than we know what category in which to put them. Hopefully, they'll make you laugh, too, in public, so people ask you what's so funny and then you can show them this book and suggest they buy their own copy.

All the News That Doesn't Fit

Bluff News Story   1) Here are three religions trying to get official recognition somewhere in the world. One is real, the other two have no believers, no dogma, not even a plate to pass around. Your job is to figure out the real one.

A) If 8,000 New Zealanders write in "Jedi" as their religion on their national census forms, the creed will become an officially recognized faith. The people behind this effort use the screenplays from George Lucas' *Star Wars* films as their scripture and center their faith on the idea of the

Force, which is "an energy field created by all living things," in the words of the sage character Obi Wan Kenobi. The Jedi believers discuss the Force in the context of theological problems, such as "should Jedi work for government?" One *Star Wars* fan told the BBC, "If George Lucas turned this into a religion, it would blow L. Ron Hubbard's *Dianetics* out of the window!"

B) Worshippers in Upper Door County, Wisconsin, have developed a provincial variation on the traditional snake-handling churches in the south. The First Church of the Living Earth compels its congregation to handle badgers as part of its weekly liturgy. Badger handling is an old Wisconsin tradition dating back to the Indians who saw the nasty burrowing creature as the lost children of the Earth Goddess. During the service, each adult celebrant comes forward to the altar and raises the badger as high as he or she can reach. "It's a demonstration of how we move from the bowels of earth to the heights of heaven," explains Reverend P. Henry Castleman.

C) For two out of five Americans today, teeth grinding is a chronic complaint. Dentists and psychotherapists do what they can to treat it, but to a growing number of communicants, teeth grinding is the fulfillment of Biblical prophecy, "There shall be weeping and wailing and gnashing of teeth." In California alone, there are now more than a dozen congregations of teeth grinders. "We are not 'holy grinders,'" says a spokesman for the sect. "We do not 'speak in teeth,' but we do take widespread gnashing as a sign that the last days are at hand."

Pick One **2) Manufacturers of early commercial ketchups used borax, scraped from dry lake beds in the California desert, as a preservative. Congress appointed Dr. Harvey Wiley to find out if it was safe. How did he go about his research?**

A) He poured ketchup on a fresh Polish sausage, encased it in glass, and watched the ketchup eat all the way through it in 4 days.

B) He subsisted entirely on ketchup and borax-laden soda crackers for a month, then presented Congress with X-rays of his perforated intestine.

C) He fed borax-laden foods to a group of strapping young men called the Poison Squad and collected all their secretions for analysis.

3) Which of these is an actual scientific device used in the manufacture of ketchup?

A) The Bostwick consistometer

B) The Luella marinating centrifugal hotpot

C) The Loyle unified pulverizor/extruder

4) Scientists and psychologists have wondered about the seemingly universal appeal of ketchup. Which of these was the reason put forward by Ernest Dichter, author of *The Psychology of Everyday Living*?

A) Much as our primitive ancestors marked their territory with scent, we mark our food by spraying liquid onto it.

B) The combination of sour vinegar and sweet sugar appeals to our need to be punished while we experience pleasure.

C) Pouring red sauce on meat makes it look raw and freshly killed, thereby increasing our sense of virility and power.

Answers on Pg. 171

Bluff News Story

5) Here are three stories of tributes—well-meaning gestures of respect gone awry. One is real, but the others are the falsest kind of praise imaginable. It's up to you to pick the real one.

A) A memorial laboratory dedicated to the late Marie Curie was closed down when it was discovered that the place had become dangerously radioactive. In an attempt accurately to honor the brilliant physicist, the organizers of the memorial had included a small amount of radium, the discovery of which made Curie and her husband, Pierre, famous. Just prior to opening the small museum in Curie's hometown, however, it became obvious that the containment vessel in which the radium had been kept was perilously inadequate. An examination of the entire building discovered high levels of radioactivity in most of the exhibits. "In a way," sighs Jean Paul Passepartout, the chairman of the organizing committee, "I think Madame might have been amused by this."

B) The late Sonny Bono, actor, singer and congressman, has been honored by the city of Palm Springs with a new statue. His widow, Mary Bono, and a friend commissioned the work, but some townsfolk don't think much of it. "It doesn't look like him," said gallery owner Dario Jones. "When I look at the statue, it looks like a crotchety old man who doesn't belong in the plaza." The statue, which sits atop the fountain, portrays Bono wearing a huge grin and stretching his hands outward. The artist, Emmanuil Snitkovsky, said he initially wanted to depict Bono the way he looked in the 1960s but was asked to sculpt a more recent image. Even former Mayor Frank Bogart, objects to the statue, but for a different reason. "I don't like it," says Bogart. "I don't think he did anything for the city. He was a lousy mayor."

C) "Funny, You Don't Look Sixty" sounded like a great TV concept: an all-star network tribute to Barbra Streisand on her 60th birthday, with guest appearances by her leading men including Robert Redford, Kris Kristofferson, George Segal, Omar Sharif, Gene Hackman, and Ryan O'Neal. There was even talk of a cameo by Bill Clinton. But Streisand, through a spokesperson, put the kibosh on the special, saying, "Ms. Streisand does not believe, at this moment in history, that calendar-age issues are in the national interest."

Pick One   6) Surfers are constantly making up new words. The first rule about surf speak is that it changes all the time. Which of these is offered as a rule of thumb, when discussing surfing conditions with surfers?

A) Modify every adjective with "way," as in, "That wave was way big."

B) End each statement with an upward inflection, as in, "Hey, the waves are really big?"

C) Use any term that could also be used to describe breakfast cereal.

7) Waves have many parts to them—the inside, outside, curl, break. Which of these is a term for a part of a wave or kind of wave?

A) A Clinton—a wave with white water

B) Jersey special—a wave that contains floating garbage

C) A Costner—a wave that looks good but doesn't move you

8) You don't see this often in surf movies, but one of the occasional side effects of surfing is motion sickness, which often results in what we "Ho-dads," or nonsurfers, call losing your lunch. What do surfers call it?

A) Talking to the seals

B) Repainting your board

C) Bowing before the great Kahuna

Answers on Pg. 171

Fill in the Blank

9) A Nevada resident turned over a package to authorities when he found that it contained _____.

10) A diner at a restaurant in Orlando _____ when the restaurant caught fire.

11) Firefighters in Richford, New York, had trouble saving Theodore Slaughter from his burning house because he was _____.

Bluff News Story

12) It doesn't take much business sense to realize that there's money to be made convincing CEOs to buy something that'll make their life easier. Here are three stories of the latest must-have executive accessories. One is real; the other two have yet to show up in the Sharper Image catalog. Your job? Pick the real one.

A) A number of plastic surgeons say that American businessmen are seeking the forceful, trustworthy profile that only a chin implant can give, at least to those who aren't naturally strong-jawed. "People with weak chins are perceived as weak characters," says California surgeon Brent Mulkin. This has spilled over from film to industry with executives and even salesmen who feel that a strong chin would enhance their credibility. The implant procedure costs about $2,500. Most feel that it's a reasonable price for the deal-making charisma and confidence their new chin will give them.

B) The latest craze in business accessories is the Sharpshooter, owing its lineage to those spring-loaded in-sleeve devices used by less-ethical poker players in the Old West. The Sharpshooter instantly snaps a business card into the hand of its wearer, adding a touch of flair to the age-old card exchange ritual. Laurel Hart, president of Powerpharnalia, Inc., says that she came up with the idea when she read that some Wall Street hotshots were buying up the genuine antique cheating de-

Answers on Pgs. 171–172

vices for just that purpose. Ms. Hart says the Sharpshooter has rapidly become their best-selling product and she expects to sell 50,000 of them by year's end.

C) It used to be that a male corporate executive would pride himself on his sharp-looking female assistant, whom he would introduce as "my gal Friday" or "the one who really runs things around here." But big-biz speak has found a new vogue expression to refer to a right-hand person. The in thing these days is to have a wise, old, male assistant, preferably one who is shorter and balder than the boss, and to introduce him as follows: "I'd like you to meet my Cheney."

Limerick   **13) The term "green thumb" isn't a joke.**
The fern likes it, as does the oak.
Go from stem to the tip.
And be loose with your grip,
For plants love a sensitive _____.

14) As he leaned back to get his head oiled
The boss said, "I was pampered, not soiled.
I am head enchilada
And was not denied nada,
I guess you might say I was _____."

Pick One   **15) We know that Shriners do good works—the burn hospitals, the free care for destitute children—but if they want us to take them seriously, they're going to have to explain the fez. What event led to the founding of the Shriners in the 1870s?**

A) The founder had a vision—sometimes ascribed to peyote—of a mystical Arabic sheik magically healing sick children.

B) A group of Masons decided that being a Mason was too boring, and decided to spice things up.

C) A Manhattan haberdasher invented the society so he could sell an oversupply of Persian fezzes.

16) Which of these was once an actual initiation ritual endured by novice Shriners?

A) Being driven 10 miles out into the countryside wearing only a fez—although they could place the fez anywhere they liked

B) Having to strip to their underwear and walk across an electrified mat symbolizing the Sahara

C) Kissing an actual camel

17) Minnesota was recently named the most caring state, with more of its citizens working overtime to provide assistance to each other. Which of these is a real example of Minnesotans going the extra mile?

A) The Cup O' Justice cafe in Ranier, Minnesota, where patrons can get genuine legal advice along with their cappuccinos

B) The Dial-A-Cheer service in Anoka, Minnesota, where people can call a toll-free number to be told nice things about themselves

C) The Hunters Counseling Center in Ely, Minnesota, where anybody who feels guilty about killing a deer or walleye can go talk about it

Bluff News Story **18) Here are three stories of jokes that somehow went awry. One is real, but the other two are merely jests themselves. It's up to you to pick the real one.**

A) The FBI is quite tough-skinned these days, but in the days of J. Edgar Hoover, the Bureau took slights very personally. According to a 1951 FBI memo, one of the things that didn't amuse Hoover at all was *Mad* magazine. When *Mad* printed an "Official Draft Dodger" card, which was to be mailed to Hoover, the FBI contacted *Mad* to voice their displeasure. *Mad*'s publisher, William Gaines, assured the Bureau in a letter that they wouldn't satirize the FBI again. In 1960 though, another irritated FBI memo proves that Mr. Gaines was ". . . obviously insincere in his promise." The Bureau complained about an "allegedly humorous advertisement-like item pertaining to J. Edgar Hoover tonic as well as a fake vacuum cleaner ad for the ' . . . Honorable J. Edgar Electrolux.'" Needless to say, the FBI's file continued to fatten for years.

B) The Statue of Liberty, according to a biography of Edward Le Bouillet, was meant as a joke. It was Le Bouillet, a French historian, who in 1865 proposed that the French join with Americans to create a statue commemorating both countries' revolutions. But La Bouillet was disdainful of the American Revolution, which he found "bourgeois and banal compared to the French one." When asked in a public forum whether American Revolutionaries had not been an inspiration to the French, he replied, "Oh, yes, of course, let's build a monument to both and let the Americans keep it." He was appalled when his sarcastic proposal was taken at face value. Ten years later, Miss Liberty stood in the New York Harbor. Ironically, Le Bouillet once wrote that "Americans have no history, because they have no irony."

C) Actress Dorothy Hildebrand is mad at just about everybody in New York acting circles. Seems that Dorothy was pretty depressed about turning 50, so friends of the actress and singer decided to cheer her up with a big surprise party. The theme was, of course, the popular "over the hill," complete with black crêpe, gravestones, and old lady jokes. But the guest of honor was less than pleased. In fact, she filed a lawsuit against the hosts; her agent of 20 years, Derek Morrison; and the owners of the Soho theatre collective where the party was held. Hildebrand's lawsuit claims that the public disclosure of her age has damaged her ability to be cast in certain roles and that the tombstones and jokes caused psychological distress and recurring nightmares.

Answers on Pg. 173

19) A big problem in Antarctica was solved with a ship-ment of two _____.

20) Cardinal Francis George of Chicago delivered a blessing at a _____, asking for the individuals gathered to respect justice and charity, and en-couraged those around him to work "for the common good."

21) Fashionable New Yorkers are going ga-ga over desserts featuring _____, a spicy ingredient showing up on the menus of finer restau-rants.

22) According to the *San Francisco Chronicle*, the Defense Department is trying to perfect the _____ via high-tech means.

23) Researchers found that you can lower your blood pressure by being around _____.

24) The contortionist's down on his luck.
"My act wound up running amuck.
Right foot on left shoulder.
Okay. There. Now hold 'er.
But I can't get it down 'cuz I'm _____."

25) "Sometimes it gets, like, annoying because, like, you can, like, smell, like, the fumes, like, during P. E. and stuff."

Bluff News Story 26) **What is one person's instant trash is another person's prize collection. Here are three stories of unusual collectibles. One is actually being hoarded and treasured by some obsessed person, but the other two are still unappreciated. It's up to you to guess the real one.**

A) Lydia Klein of Overland Park, Kansas, has a closet full of America Online CDs, the ones that come free in the mail. "I think AOL is a huge part of our pop culture," she says. Some disks just have the AOL logo but others are backed with myriad graphic images of palm trees, bubble gum, clouds, even Casper the Friendly Ghost. Many of them are rare. Klein has a disk from 1989 and has paid anywhere from $30 to $54 for a find. AOL employees collect as well, and they won't say how many thousands, perhaps millions, are out there.

B) Lawrence O'Connor of Irvine, California, believes he has the world's largest collection of airsickness bags. He has more than 300 of them from obscure foreign carriers to airlines that no longer exist, like Freddy Laker's Laker Airways. Occasionally, when he's heard that an airline is about to go under, like Eastern, he's booked a short flight just to get his hands on the remaining bags. He said he became fascinated with them on a business flight when he realized that no matter how advanced aviation gets, people are still biologically cavemen. If such a thing exists, he says he would love a Presidential barf bag from Air Force One and that he would be willing to vote for the candidate who would send him one.

C) Quentin Driswell of Milwaukee is building a room onto his house to showcase his extensive collection of badminton shuttlecocks. Driswell, 52, is a lifelong badminton fanatic and has spanned the globe collecting shuttlecocks used in various world and Olympic championship events. His collection includes a shuttlecock once used on the White House lawn by Theodore Roosevelt, another used by the children of Czar Nicholas II, and one taken to the moon by the crew of Apollo 15. "Call me crazy," Driswell says, "but whatever you do, don't ever call these things birdies."

Answers on Pgs. 173–174

Limerick

27) If your brain doesn't meet high demands
Here's some gestures to loosen your glands.
Put 'em up in the air
Shake 'em like you don't care
You'll be smarter if you use your _____.

Fill in the Blank

28) An updated edition of the Oxford English Dictionary includes a new word that's defined as "Expressing frustra-
tion at the realization that things have turned out badly or
not as planned, or that one has just said or done something foolish." This
familiar, one-syllable word is _____.

29) Hasbro Toy executives have been patrolling the streets and parks of
Chicago looking for _____.

30) A California health insurer denied coverage to a teenager because his
_____ made him too much of a medical risk.

Bluff News Story

31) Here are three stories about keeping clean. One is real,
but the other two are grimy untruths. It's up to you to pick
the real one.

A) A book about the legendary eccentric Howard Hughes contains details
about his obsession with cleanliness and casts doubt on the name of the
mammoth plane that was one of his great legacies. Biographer Ann Dinges
reveals that the billionaire aviator was so afraid of germs and disease
that he swaddled himself in layers of clothing. Dinges discovered letters written by Hughes to his personal secretary that mention 60-

Answers on Pg. 175

day supplies of mosquito netting, rubber gloves, and face masks made of the most impervious Chinese silk. "Most days he looked like an Afghan woman in a very expensive burka," says Dinges. As for the plane Hughes built—the world's largest at the time, with a 320-foot wingspan—Dinges challenges the conventional wisdom that it was called the Spruce Goose. "He had maids mopping and disinfecting the floors every hour day or night, even when the plane wasn't in use. It was so clean that it came to be known as the Spruced Goose. How the history books got it wrong, we'll never know."

B) Giving your dog or cat a bath is often a traumatic experience for both pet and owner. But all of that will soon change thanks to the Lavakon, an automatic washing machine for cats and dogs. The side-loading washer is the invention of Eduardo Segura and Andres Diaz of Spain, who hope to sell their machines to animal grooming shops. The Lavakon stands acts like an animal-size car wash and is equipped with a series of nozzles that gently massage your pet with soap and water. Pet groomers are already itching to get their hands on the Lavakon. Carlos Sewer of Petclean USA plans to launch a chain of pet launderettes. He says, "It's really unbelievable. You have to see how clean it gets the dogs. Even those with long hair."

C) Just in time for those cozy but environmentally correct winter nights: clean firewood. We are talking about wood that has been organically treated to eliminate toxins. Derek Small and Wendy Rieger of San Jose, California, have developed what they call mink wood, or wood that has been cleaned with mink urine. Two years ago, Small was given free wood from the grounds of a neighboring mink farm. When he burned the logs using his wood stove, they burned longer and cleaner than any logs he had ever used. Small and Rieger did some research and now say that firewood dipped in mink urine cuts smoke in half and releases virtually no harmful chemicals into the atmosphere.

32) "I don't give a (bleep) that your family goes back to pre-Revolutionary times and you've got more wealth than I could imagine. If it's no good, I'm going to say so."

Fill in the Blank

33) Two police officers in Albuquerque, New Mexico, were investigated after they used their police helicopter to _____.

34) A man in Kentucky told police he received a gunshot wound in his leg while fighting a duel with _____.

Answers on Pgs. 175–176

Answers

Animals

1) Answer: Waddle. It may look ridiculous to us leggy Homo sapiens, but for the Emperor penguin, waddling is the ideal form of locomotion. A study in the journal *Nature* reports that the awkward side-to-side gait is the most efficient, if inelegant, method of walking for the penguin.

2) Answer: Wimp. A research paleontologist in Wyoming says that the fiercest of all dinosaurs, the bloodthirsty Tyrannosaurus Rex, was really nothing more than a timid schlemiel. Robert Bakker bases his theory on cracks and holes in fossilized T-Rex bones. Says Bakker, "They were beat-up, limping, had oozing sores, and were disease-

Carl Kasell

ridden. Even worse," he adds, "if we did Jurassic Park 4, T-Rex would be portrayed as a large Woody Allen character."

3) Answer: Stuffed. Gray Taxidermy of Pompano Beach, Florida, was cited by the state Attorney General for using unfair business practices. Apparently, they paid fishing boat captains to pressure their clients to get their catches mounted—immediately! Right now!—even if they were little tiny things. The fish-stuffing outfit is being fined, and boat captains will have to follow an ethics code.

4) Answer: Ate. An endangered leatherback sea turtle had been injured in the wild by a boat and was brought to the Seaquarium for treatment. Sadly, it died the same day. An employee from a Caribbean island, where eating turtles is common, removed some meat to make stew, which he brought in for lunch the next day. Says an environmentalist critic, "His is just the absolute height of stupidity. We're changing the name to the Miami Seaquarium & Barbecue." The Seaquarium has promised not to eat any more of its animals.

5) Answer: Deer. Carole Moore's five grandkids are still laughing over Ms. Moore's Christmastime encounter with a white-tailed buck. She was standing along a street in New Braunfels, Texas, near her husband, who was sitting in their van, when BAM! A deer ran by and clipped her, knocking her over. Ms. Moore was shaken but not injured. Harold Moore said he was so amazed by his wife's one-in-a-million encounter that he went out and bought a lottery ticket.

6) Answer: Silent. They held the contest anyway. The winning rooster crowed twice, beating the only other rooster to make a sound. State Fair officials blame the heat for the lack of crowing. Bird owners made sounds, poked cages, and flapped their arms, but to no avail. One owner said, "I can't understand it. He crows all the time, but you bring him here and all of a sudden he gets shy."

7) Answer: B. The Aboistop is an electronic device that hangs on the dog's collar. When the dog barks, the box lets loose a spray of citronella, which distracts the dog.

8) Answer: Swim. According to a memo distributed by the British Ministry of Agriculture, Fisheries and Food, cod don't swim particularly well, so, "they are easily overtaken by trawlers and nets." The memo has a number of interesting facts about North Sea cod, gleaned from observations of Dennis, a captive cod the Ministry has kept for 18 years.

9) Answer: Raccoon. The annual coon feed in Delafield, Wisconsin, was cancelled because of a severe shortage of raccoons. Organizers, blaming an unusually cold early winter, were able to come up with only 10 of the 100 needed varmints for the feast. By the way, Delafielders say that raccoon tastes just like beef.

10) Answer: Laugh. After years of debate and speculation, it has been confirmed that dogs laugh. Dr. Patricia Simonet discovered the dog laughs, which sound like "huh-huh," while recording canines in a park. She's says that dogs don't respond to, say, one-liners about Chihuahuas, but to the sounds of other dogs laughing. To test her theory, Dr. Simonet played a cassette of dogs huh-huhing to some puppies and they playfully rolled on the floor and yipped. A cassette of a Joe Piscopo stand-up routine resulted in quizzical doggy looks and frightened whimpers.

11) Answer: Steak. After 3 years of tireless and delicious research, meat scientists at the Universities of Nebraska and Florida have discovered a new kind of steak. They call it the flat iron and it's said to be as tasty as a New York strip, but at a Salisbury steak price. The flat iron is cut from the difficult-to-reach shoulder area, same as your inexpensive chuck steak.

12) Answer: Beavers. Tallahassee County officials and local builders have been trying to rid a development site of the bucktoothed rodents. Workers repeatedly tore down the dams but the creatures just rebuilt them. (It's what beavers do.) Finally, the construction company found what appears to be beaver Kryptonite: rock music. Continually blaring guitar riffs have driven out the critters once and for all.

13) Answer: A poodle. A lawyer filed suit against a veterinarian on behalf of Poopi the poodle and her owners. Poopi went to the vet for a tooth cleaning but the vet allegedly tried to spay the dog.

14) Answer: Arnold the crime-fighting pig. Last year, Becky Moyer was held up by two men outside her home in Minneapolis. She told the criminals that her purse was in the house. After luring the criminals inside, she yelled for her 300-pound pet pig. Arnold grabbed one of the robbers by the leg, who shouted, "There's a —ing pig in here!" before fleeing with his partner.

15) Answer: Petting Great White sharks. South Australia Environment Minister Iain Evans is asking his department to consider rules requiring people to keep their distance from dead whales as well as live ones after a group of tourists were caught on tape climbing onto a dead whale and petting the noses of Great White sharks who were feeding on it. Evans said, "These creatures are not toys. It is clear that the state government will need to look at changing the law in order to protect people who are too stupid to protect themselves."

16) Answer: A. The whirring sound made by a female mosquito's wings is one of the only ways a male mosquito can find her. Mosquitoes can be sexually active by the time they're 2 days old, and though we won't go into detail, suffice it to say that the male's lot is not a happy one. Incidentally, the mosquitoes that bite are female.

17) Answer: A. The cartoon characters appeared in the military newspaper *Stars and Stripes*. Armed Forces Radio broadcast so many anti-malaria messages that troops began calling it "the mosquito network."

18) Answer: Lose. British racehorse Quixall Crossett earns the love of his many fans because of his indomitable failure to win. Informally called Champion the Blunder Horse, the spry 16-year-old lost his 100th consecutive race, not even bothering to finish, actually, but enjoying the roar of the crowd. His doting owners, Ted and Joy Caine, said he seemed to be having fun.

19) Answer: Arms. If octopuses weren't creepy enough, it turns out they have brains in their arms. Scientists in Israel were trying to determine how an octopus could coordinate eight flailing tentacles. The answer: eight separate nervous systems in the appendages. Basically, this means that the octopus sends the move command to its arms and they simply take over.

20) Answer: Rogers. Dog breeder Karin Klouman claims the secret to getting her golden retrievers aroused lies in the "calm relaxed tones" of Mr. Rogers. In the past, Ms. Klouman relied on the sonorous cooing of newscasters such as

Peter Jennings and Dan Rather to put her dogs in the mood, but some headlines are proving to be a distraction. She told Canada's *McLean's* magazine, "The dogs can sense when the news is upsetting."

21) Answer: Pet rabbit. Firefighters suspect that Cinnamon, a bunny, caused the fire by gnawing on a clothes dryer's electrical cord. Susan Mitchell, the bunny's owner, thinks it was the dryer's fault, not the bunny's. However, the fire chief believes that no matter what the result of the investigation, Cinnamon should not be allowed to chew on any more electrical cords.

22) Answer: Turtle. A 17-year-old turtle, in fact. Max Schell—get it?—lives in a tank in Stefanie McLaughlin's apartment in Boston, where he received his jury summons. Says McLaughlin, quote, "Max might be well-suited to jury duty. There's a lot of sitting around and waiting involved. He's very good at that."

23) Answer: C. "If you're not paying attention and you hear that sound, you think it's what it's mimicking. So, you hear a phone ringing and then suddenly you realize that it's a bird making that sound or you hear the sound of brakes on a big truck and it's coming out of a bird," says Doug Stotz, an ornithologist at the Field Museum in Chicago.

24) Answer: Shrimp. All is not well at the aquarium in Monterey, California. A 3½-inch shrimp, of the smasher mantis variety, is terrorizing a tank full of snails and hermit crabs. The cunning crustacean uses a powerful calcified claw to smash through shells and rocks. Aquarium officials blame the loss of barnacles, crabs, and at least two fire fish on the shrimp. And aquarium officials are not taking this lightly. Said one, "I got a letter from a surgeon in South Africa who saw a 10-inch-long smasher. When he tried to grab it, it so severely damaged his finger that they had to amputate."

25) Answer: Steer. The New Mexico State Fair Agricultural Committee is considering a "blow and show" rule that would limit the dressing up of blue-ribbon bovines to a shampoo and blow-dry only. This means no more clipping, contouring, hair coloring, or wigs.

26) Answer: Chimp. Chippy, an 11-year-old chimp at the Blair Drummond Safari Park in Stirling, Scotland, managed to steal a cell phone from his keeper's jacket and used it to repeatedly speed-dial three employees for two consecutive nights. The staffers all reported an anonymous caller who breathed or made "strange snuffling" noises on the line. Finally, one employee yelled into the phone and was answered by a loud shriek. Zoo officials think Chippy must have seen staff and visitors using their cell phones and mimicked the calling behavior.

27) Answer: Spawn. Thanks to the tireless efforts of the gang at the National Board of Fisheries in Sweden, we now know that female trout occasionally fake orgasms. Apparently, all the violent quivering, the rush of bubbles out of puffing gills, is an act put on to attract more males—hopefully including one with signs of genetic superiority, such as a nice set of fins or a large jaw. Scientists also observed several female trout passing out tiny cocktail napkins with fake phone numbers.

28) Answer: Beavers. Those hardworking, bucktoothed engineers of the animal kingdom are overrunning Canada, flooding fields and cutting down valuable trees. The beaver is officially recognized by Queen Elizabeth as symbol of the sovereignty of the dominion of Canada, but apparently she has not seen headlines like BEAVERS OUT OF CONTROL or CRAZED BEAVER TERRIFIES FARM PETS. The Canadian Wildlife Service has issued a warning saying that if threatened, "Beavers rear up on their hind legs, and loudly hiss or growl, before lunging forward to deliver extremely damaging bites." In response, the Service has issued a travel advisory to Americans saying if they're going to Canada, not to wear wood.

29) Answer: B. Certain species of ants are entirely dependent on labor provided by slave species, which they capture in raids and carry over their shoulders back to their nests.

30) Answer: B. These South American ants have developed a supersize gland that runs the length of their bodies. When sufficiently provoked, they start twitching violently until they blow up, showering their enemy with sticky goo.

31) Answer: A tortoise. Officials at the Animal Crackers Farm Zoo in Greenville, Michigan, say they thought they would find Big Bertha, the tortoise, pretty quickly, but apparently, she was moving at her top speed of a mile every 2 days and she eluded them. Zoo owner Judith Lepew admits that they should never have taken their eyes off the little scamp.

32) Answer: Cook himself dinner. While the Lemme family was at church, Bear, their 13-year-old chocolate lab, decided he needed a little snack. Bear apparently knocked a 5-pound bag of dog food onto the stove and then somehow managed to turn it on. When the Lemmes returned home, the house was full of smoke, charred kibble littered the floor, and Bear was huddled in a basement corner. Said Lori Lemme, "This 70-pound dog has trouble getting off the couch, but when it comes to food, he can do miracles."

33) Answer: Humpback whales. Specifically, Western Australian humpback whales. The journal *Nature* reported that about 2,000 humpbacks off the east coast of Australia have been singing the same 10-minute mating song, with only slight variations, for over 2 decades. But in 1996, two male humpbacks from the western side of the continent made their way over and began singing their own distinctive song. Researchers thought the new song would quickly be overshadowed, but it actually became an undersea hit, as the eastern whales dropped their old song and started imitating the new one. Researchers suspect that the western song—not just new, but very loud—was extremely popular with the ladies.

34) Answer: Fall over when planes fly over them. Ever since pilots started reporting the phenomena during the Falklands War, it's been believed that if you fly a plane over a flock of penguins, the birds will all look up and then back, back, back until they topple over on their derrieres. So the Royal Navy spent about $36,000 to fly some helicopters over penguins in Antarctica to see what would happen. Some penguins ran away, but none of them ever fell over.

35) Answer: C. Freeze-drying pets has become fairly popular among pet owners and taxidermists because it's much less complicated and expensive than traditional taxidermy. One freeze-dried pet owner told the *Wall Street Journal*, "This way, I can always look at him and kiss him goodnight."

36) Answer: C. It takes place near Milan and it draws spectators from all over the continent. This year, the grand prize is six piglets, while the second and third prizes are two ostriches and 500 eggs, respectively. It should be noted that simple slaying isn't good enough. Each tiny corpse must be saved and produced for the judge's inspection.

37) Answer: Squid. A 550-pound giant squid described by scientists as "one of the last true monsters of the deep" was recently discovered off the coast of Melbourne, Australia. Including its two feeding tentacles, the creature is over 36 feet long and would produce calamari the size of a car tire. As delicious as that sounds, the giant squid have ammonia pockets in their flesh that would give the creature a certain Lysol-like taste.

38) Answer: Donkey. Geoff Roder is going to have to find another mode of transport when going to the drive-in. The New Zealand bachelor's preferred ride, his faithful donkey companion, has been banned from the theater because it blocks the view of other moviegoers. Says cinema manager Mike Burnside, "I like Geoff, but I've told him 100 times to leave the donkey at home."

39) Answer: Disney. In an effort to promote a better understanding of irony, Disney has begun using birds of prey to hunt mice at one of its theme parks. Disney's California Adventure Park is loading up on large birdhouses to attract hawks and owls in the hopes they will feast on the rodents attacking the park's Robert Mondavi vineyard. Of course, the symbol of Disney's international empire of fun is a mouse. Says a spokesman for the winery, "We—heh, heh—we hope Mickey survives. I'd hate to see an owl after Mickey."

40) Answer: Turkey. Tim Hoban's complaints were met with laughter and gobbling noises from his colleagues until supervisors went along on the route to check out the savage bird. "Their jaws just dropped," he said. George, the wild turkey, flaps, screams, and lunges beak-first. Said the mailman, "He's an attack dog. He's really scary. He's got feet bigger than my hands." Higher-ups have stated that George is the first turkey to ever interfere with the U. S. mail and he will be stopped.

41) Answer: Recognize themselves. All sorts of animals look in mirrors, but in what's being billed as a major discovery, it's now believed dolphins actually know they are looking at themselves. Biologists used to think that only primates had the intelligence to recognize themselves in a mirror; now biologist Diana Reiss has added dolphins to that list. Reiss found that when she marked Xs on some dolphins and placed them in front of a mirror, they started jumping and spinning in the tank trying to get a look at themselves and the marks.

42) Answer: Cod. This heartwarming fish tale from Norway is about a kind-hearted fisherman and a blind cod. Harald Hauso has caught the same scrawny fish 40 times in his nets, but this time decided not to throw it back. Instead, the cod was transported in a large tank to a marine park where he will share a private pool with a short-sighted halibut known as Big Mama. Says the Norwegian, "I'll take a trip to visit him there if he survives."

43) Answer: Hair. Researchers at Colorado State University have discovered that you can tell a lot about a cow by the way he coifs his hair. Cows with a little curl between the eyes, known to bovine stylists as the facial whorl, tend to be of an even temperament, while those bulls with no curl or a curl high on their heads are often rascally and agitated.

44) Answer: Crows. Tokyo is being overrun by crows. About 30,000 of them, to be exact. With no natural enemies and all sorts of garbage for them to feast on, the black-winged menace is taking over the city. Horror stories of crows attacking people are common and their habit of nesting on power lines has caused at least five blackouts. Not to worry, the governor of Tokyo has a plan: eat them. He's declared his intentions to make crow-meat pies Tokyo's special dish.

45) Answer: C. The drink and dump behavior, as it were, can be triggered by as little as 2 milliliters of water in the ants' nest.

Business

1) Answer: B. "There are over 50 million sandwiches made to eat in a week in England, which equals 2.2 billion sandwiches a year, so it's actually a very successful industry, and with the name Earl of Sandwich, why were they the only ones who weren't tapping into this successful market?" says Jasmine Pelham, the publicity agent for the Earl of Sandwich.

2) Answer: A. The digital fry pan has a little keypad and display in the handle. You input what you're cooking and how you want it cooked, and it lets you know when to put the food on and when it should be done. A 10-inch model will cost $90.

3) Answer: C. "The difference between the hair prosthesis and something that you go to the store and buy is the fact that these places measure your scalp, they take samples of your hair, and they try to match to it with natural hair. And it's made special for you. Not everybody can wear it. Some of these places that you go to, ready-made places, anybody can wear them. This is made special for the individual," according to Pennsylvania State Representative Anthony DeLuca, the sponsor of the hairpiece bill, which he assures us we should take very seriously. And for those who are wondering, Mr. DeLuca has a full head of hair.

4) Answer: The human stomach.

5) Answer: The stock market.

6) Answer: Wal-Mart. Some call it "boondocking," but we prefer to call it what it really is—camping overnight in Wal-Mart parking lots. The Dallas morning news reports that boondocking or "dry camping" is all the rage among the RV/bargain-hunting set. Says Wal-Mart spokesman Tom Williams, "It is the natural marriage of a store open 24 hours that has a big parking lot and the freedom that RVs give." Plus, he did not go on to say, they beautify our stores by preventing people from seeing them.

7) Answer: B. The inventor of the Snore Stopper says that the electric shock isn't enough to wake you, it's just enough to make you change position and stop snoring. It costs $40, but, says its maker, for the person next to you, it's price-less.

8) Answer: B. "Well, Yahoo Serious was supposed to make a big splash in the United States, uh, unfortunately, for Yahoo, he didn't really become a big deal in America, and his last movie, *Mr. Accident*, never even got released in the U. S.," says *Chicago Tribune* film writer Mark Caro, telling us about the film career, such as it has been, of Mr. Yahoo Serious, who is in fact suing Yahoo.com.

9) Answer: Cigarette butts. To get a sense of the situation, the *Times* talked not to the financial titans, but the people who clean up after them— the street sweepers, janitors, and shoe-shine people. They report that the cigarette butts they're picking up are shorter, meaning that brokers have more time to smoke them, meaning that the market is sinking. Office cleaners say that there's less work to do as financial firms lay off brokers. The worst indicator: a broker asking the guy shining his shoes for stock tips.

10) Answer: Tax refunds. A few examples of Dr. Cooper's federal tax break plan are the following: If you keep your body mass index under 25, you'll get a $250.00 deduction . . . and the same goes for keeping your blood pressure under 140 over 90. You'll also get $250 back if you don't smoke and keep your cholesterol level under 200. No word yet if the Thighmaster will be tax de-ductible.

11) Answer: Love Thy Neighbor. Florida's Love Thy Neighbor is a small, family-run charitable organization that helps the homeless. Michigan's Love Thy Neighbor is a company that sells jewelry and trinkets under a variety of names. The Florida guy says the Michigan woman has been bugging him for years, and just wants his Web site address, www.lovethyneighbor.org. When asked by the Detroit *Free Press* how a Florida charity could in any way be confused with a Michigan retailer, the Michigan woman said her company did do charitable work, she just couldn't remember any details at the time.

12) Answer: C. "An integral part of queuing is moaning about having to queue, and as everyone knows, we all love to moan over here, um, especially about queuing, it's just probably as important as moaning about the weather," according to Daniel Sheldon, a journalist based in London. That hatred, of course, is what Queue for You is going to try to profit from.

13) Answer: Camaro. GM first made the sports car back in 1967, and for years it's rivaled Ford's Mustang as the car that guys buy to make up for their lack of . . . I mean, to impress girls. But in the era of SUVs and 700-Series Beemers, Camaro sales have hit the skids. So GM is discontinuing the Camaro as well as the Firebird. Val McClatchey was so impressed by her date's 1968 Camaro that she bought her own and later founded the Keystone Camaro Club. She offered some fightin' words for Mustang fans, saying that the Chevrolet sports car will "beat the pants off" the Ford in a race.

14) Answer: Taliban. The former rulers of Afghanistan may have hated anything more technically advanced than a mallet, but they loved to travel in style: in Toyota Hilux pickup trucks, and for Osama bin Laden and his highly placed lieutenants, luxury Land Cruiser SUVs. Toyota hastens to assure us that there is no "Mid-Kabul Toyota City," or any licensed dealer anywhere in the country . . . all of the vehicles were smuggled in illegally.

15) Answer: C. "One question that we do get asked quite a lot is, 'Are the shopping boyfriends gay?' I have to say that no, the two boyfriends that we had, they weren't gay, but they just loved shopping and were very enthusiastic about it," says Pauline Shaw, Marketing Associate from the Braehead Shopping Center in Glasgow, Scotland.

16) Answer: Car. This week, Sony Corporation, creators of Aibo the robotic dog, and Toyota unveiled the first car that can feel. It's called the Pod and it's possibly the first car ever created outside of Disney that can smile, cry flashing blue tears, and wag its tail. When the Pod's owner approaches, it lights up bright orange and yellow. And once on the road, the Pod reacts to the driver's mood. If it senses agitation, for example, it will play calming music and blow cool air.

17) Answer: Cracker. To celebrate the product's 100th birthday, the folks at Barnum Animal Crackers added another animal to their roster of tasty cookies. Four animals contended to take the spot of 18th animal cracker: the koala bear, the walrus, the penguin, and the cobra. The penguin took an early lead after a strong showing in the talent and evening wear competitions, but the eventual winner was the koala.

18) Answer: SPAM. SPAM, of course, is the famous spongy pink luncheon meat made by Hormel. It's also a word used to describe all the unsolicited e-mail zinging around the Internet, inviting you to visit porn sites or make lots of dollar bill signs in your home. Hormel tried to stop people from using the term, but has now admitted that it's too widespread to stop. They merely ask that when referring to the luncheon meat, we use all capital letters.

19) Answer: Fast food. Originally, the owners of Nelson's Chicken and Gravy Land insisted that their restaurant had nothing to do with Nelson Mandela, despite their logo featuring his likeness and dishes like "Nelson's Freedom Meal" and "Nelson's Peace Meal." Eventually, however, the two men owned up, apologized to the international icon of goodness, and agreed to rename their restaurant . . . presumably to something like Pik Botha's Pik-a-Chik.

20) Answer: Sues. It's hard to be sure, but the massive retailer might be the most sued private company in America. The complaints range from the typical— people who slipped and fell in the aisles or had big boxes of toilet paper fall on their heads—to the bizarre, like the six ladies who say they were injured in riots that occurred when customers tried to get their hands on an irresponsibly small supply of Furbies. Wal-Mart, unlike some other firms, fights almost every suit, despite it often being cheaper to settle.

21) Answer: A. "The taste is characteristically very similar to Sumatran coffees, but because of the muskiness of this little creature in part, it does have a very, very unusual aftertaste, very long and full-bodied and slightly sweet," says John Martinez Jr. of J. Martinez and Company, coffee merchants in Atlanta, Georgia, purveyor of fine predigested coffee.

22) Answer: A. The ads, in which the two kidnappers play, quote, "nasty tricks" on the abducted Claus, were pulled after Sony executives decided that people "might misinterpret the edginess of the campaign."

23) Answer: The video rental business. We don't know if Adam Smith mentioned this in *The Wealth of Nations*, but one of the laws of economics seems to be that when the going gets tough, people stay home and watch videos. Everything afflicting the rest of the economy—all the bad news on the front pages, fear among consumers to spend money or travel—all combine into the overwhelming urge to run down to Blockbuster, rent the entire series of *Police Academy* movies, and hole up for a week.

24) Answer: A computer. Specifically, that wonderful musty smell of polyester that wafts from a computer's packing case. The limited-edition perfume, available only on the Internet, is designed for those people whose fondest memories involve late nights at the workstation. Jim Krivda, the perfume's designer, says, "When I open up a box of Christmas lights, it reminds me of my childhood . . . we think younger people might feel the same way about opening a box that holds a computer."

25) Answer: Mary Kay. Mary Kay Ash started selling skin care products at in-home demonstrations in 1963 and eventually built Mary Kay Cosmetics into a billion-dollar company. Her success was based in part on her system of recruiting and rewarding Mary Kay Ladies. Top sellers such as Ruth Gross Gibson of Topeka, Kansas, got themselves pink cars just like Mary Kay's own. Mary Kay once explained that she had no choice but to start her own business at the age of 45. She said, "I was middle-aged, had varicose veins, and I didn't have time to fool around."

26) Answer: Dave Thomas. The high school dropout who founded Wendy's hamburger chain became a multimillionaire, and then, late in life, a celebrity because of his 10-year run as a pitchman for his company, died in 2001 at the age of 69. People credited his success against such vicious competitors as Ronald McDonald and Herb from Burger King because a), he seemed so honest, and b) he looked like a man who had enjoyed more than a few double cheeseburgers during his lifetime. By the way, he finally did get his high school diploma, at the age of 60, and attended the senior prom at a school near his home in Florida. He was voted "Most Likely To Succeed."

Education

1) Answer: B. "They conducted seminars on learning to compromise, learning to negotiate, learning to communicate, basically, so that the anguish in deciding whether you want a plaid couch or a floral couch is diminished," says Lawrence Martaugh, public relations manager for IKEA Canada.

2) Answer: Clifton K. Hillegass, whose work directly contradicted that statement of principle. Mr. Hillegass created *Cliff's Notes*, which were life-savers for students who put off reading *Moby Dick* until the night before the quiz. Hillegass said he never intended them to become substitutes for reading the books themselves. In the *Washington Post*, Hank Steuver wrote a Cliff Note–like appreciation of Hillegass. "In his life story, themes of discipline and erudition come into conflict with ideas of modern haste and an overemphasis on quantitative grades. In a culture of how-to "Dummies" guides, the "quick fix," and the career of Freddie Prinze Jr., what are some other examples of the inherent intellectual dishonesty in man? Discuss."

3) Answer: School lunches. In a compartment behind a radiator, workers found piles of abandoned sandwiches, cartons of milk, and yogurt with expiration dates from 25 years ago. The discovery solved the mystery of the strange odors that had plagued the school.

4) Answer: B. The National Organization for the Reform of Marijuana Laws provides scholarships to students who write essays outlining what NORML calls a more sensible drug policy. One year, an essay on the Dutch model for legalizing pot resulted in a $650 scholarship for a young man named Kevin Kilo.

5) Answer: A. The Deppen Scholarship—reserved for graduates of a single high school—is known as the Goodie-Goodie Scholarship.

6) Answer: B. "It was not the calling out of the grade that the court found objectionable. It was simply the fact that another student saw another student's grade. The court made it clear that students couldn't grade the papers and they could not even collect the papers that had already been graded because then they would need to look down and see what the other students' grades were," said Michael Simpson, assistant general counsel of the National Education Association.

7) Answer: A. Young Mr. or Miss Zolp also has to be Catholic.

8) Answer: Hugging. Pequot Lakes Junior High School in Minnesota is reprimanding students for hugging. According to students, the halls are clogged with huggers. Some students claim to receive upward of 60 hugs a day. Principal Chuck Arns insists that the reprimands have more to do with tardiness and lingering between classes than hugging. "It doesn't matter why you are late," Arns said. "If it's because you are hugging, we just encourage the kids to move it along."

9) Answer: Cookie. Pennsylvania high school junior Chris Flachsbart has been suspended for making "nonserious" campaign promises. In addition to promising cookies to everyone who voted for him, Mr. Flachsbart also promises to paint the school blue and install conveyor belts in the hallways. The administration wasn't amused, however, and suspended the aspiring politico for 1 day and disqualified him from the race.

10) Answer: School lunches. The most acclaimed restaurant in Finn Rock, Oregon, is the elementary school cafeteria. Lunch lady and former gourmet chef Bernadette Fleischer would rather serve her students haute cuisine than tater tots. Rave reviews of her school lunches have local businessmen and women stopping by for meals. However, not all are thrilled at the eclectic options. According to the Associated Press, kindergartners responded to Sushi Day with "Eeeeuu! What's that?"

Entertainment

1) Answer: C. The ad executive who bought the show for Philip Morris showed the pilot to his good friend Oscar Hammerstein, who said, "Keep the redhead and ditch the Cuban. . . . And if you have to keep him, for God's sake don't let him sing." That contract provision was dropped soon after the first season.

2) Answer: A. This made the network people happy, although still, nobody could say the word "pregnant" on the show.

3) Answer: Hugh Hefner. Mr. Hefner was speaking at Oxford as part of his 75th-birthday tour of Europe. The *Playboy* magnate answered questions about the early days of the magazine, which was almost called *Stag Night*, and talked about the lack of affection he received growing up in Nebraska. He said, "When I was young I had a security blanket and a pet dog. The dog got sick and died and the blanket had to be burned, so I guess I was trying to recreate the image of security in the bunny. It was a Citizen Kane/Rosebud thing."

4) Answer: Perry Como. Como, born Pierino Como, was once a barber but starting singing with big bands back in the 1930s. He almost went back to barbering—he liked the hours better—but an agent convinced him to give singing one more try and by the 1950s, he was a huge hit-maker with a top-rated TV show. Como's style was as relaxed as they get, and his song choices were never very challenging. Among his hits: "Hubba Hubba," "Zing Zing, Zoom Zoom," "Papaya-Mama," "Hot Diggity," and "Chi-Baba, Chi-Baba."

5) Answer: Toilet.

6) Answer: A monkey. J. Fred Muggs was Dave Garroway's co-star on the *Today Show* from February 1953 to March 1957. He traveled to 42 countries as a goodwill ambassador, met with three presidents of the United States, and was debated in Parliament during the Coronation of Queen Elizabeth. After the *Today Show*, as befits a star, he got his own show on PBS, the *J. Fred Muggs Show*.

7) Answer: B. Pope was trying to find the *Enquirer's* niche among the varied papers of the day when he got caught in a traffic jam caused by people staring a fatal car wreck. He realized people love to look at murder, mayhem, and horror, and relaunched the *Enquirer* as a weekly digest of the bizarre.

8) Answer: B. The *Enquirer* completed its transformation from blood and guts gross-out stories to celebrity gossip with the change to color pictures in 1979. Pope was left with a black-and-white printing plant, so he came up with the *Weekly World News*, which was supposed to appeal to the lowest of the lowbrow audience. It succeeded: The *Weekly World News* sells more than a million copies a week.

9) Answer: C. "They will get briefings on various aspects of the program based upon their level of interest, some people are interested more in lasers, some people more so in the threat. I've seen Jeff Baxter probably a dozen times in the past five years," said Lieutenant Colonel Rick Leonard, discussing Jeff "Skunk" Baxter's involvement with the defense department and National Missile Defense.

10) Answer: C. The Brookhaven National Laboratory on Long Island scared the dickens out its neighbors, so the scientists invited people in once a year for Visitor's Day, which was boring until a scientist programmed a room-size computer to play tennis on a 5-inch screen. People lined up for hours for their turn to play.

11) Answer: B. Space Invaders was so popular in Japan, where it was invented, that it almost brought the cash economy there to a standstill.

12) Answer: B. *Maxim* does not allow the word "babe," although that word succinctly describes most of its editorial and photographic content. By the way, *Town and Country* loves the word "rich," although they frown on "affluent" and "wealthy."

13) Answer: Anthony Quinn. Because the half-Mexican, half-Irish actor looked generically ethnic to Hollywood producers, he often played the role of the foreigner, from a Bedouin prince in *Lawrence of Arabia* to Zorba the Greek. By the way, in real life he usually did get the girl, as evidenced by the closing lines from his *Los Angeles Times* obituary: "He is survived by his children: Christina,

Kathleen, Valentina, and Duncan by [his first wife]; Francesco, Daniele, and Lorenzo by [his second]; Antonia and Ryan by [his third]; Alex and Sean by an unnamed German woman, and an unnamed son by an unnamed French woman."

14) Answer: A spokesman for Barbra Streisand. The superstar, Democratic activist, and voice of moderation posted a letter on her Web site urging people to conserve energy in various ways. When asked if she herself was planning to pitch in, her spokesman first said, "You really expect me to ask her that?" and then went and got the official answer: No. According to the *New York Post*, it turns our Babs is a bit of an air-conditioning freak. A Streisand confidant told the *Post*, "She is someone who cannot be hot, not even for a minute. Maybe it's menopause, but she refuses to sweat."

15) Answer: "In Heaven There Is No Beer."

16) Answer: Men's room.

17) Answer: The Bee Gees. Students were asked to write a compulsory exam essay on themes of tragedy while considering the lines, "It's tragedy. . . . Tragedy when you lose control and you got no soul, it's tragedy," from the 1979 hit by the brothers Gibb. British education officials reacted with predictably high dudgeon. "Tragedy is part of English Literature that does not need to be soiled with pop lyrics," sniffed one. But the chairman of the English finals examination board told the *Daily Telegraph* that Bee Gees lyrics had echoes in the great central canonical texts. "'The feeling's gone and you can't go on' is a fair summary of the end of *King Lear*."

18) Answer: Steal. Mr. Cassaway is the co-curator of the "Steal This Art" exhibit at Philadelphia's Box Populi gallery. The Yippie-inspired exhibit was conceived as a way to get visitors to "interact" with the art—and after just 6 minutes of interacting, all the art was gone. Dozens of people lined up outside for the show's opening, and when the doors opened it turned into a mob scene. Even the police were called in when a piece from the gallery's permanent collection was stolen.

19) Answer: Bs. The Queen of the Bs was Marie Windsor, who died at the age 80. The *Los Angeles Times* called her the "definitive noir heroine—glamorous and dangerous" for her work in *Force of Evil* and *The Narrow Margin*. But it was a string of starring roles in movies like *Swamp Women* and *Cat Women of the Moon* that earned the former cigarette girl her crown as queen.

20) Answer: B. We can't account for the rest of it, but the gratuitous reference to Tom Wolfe goes back to one of the great literary spats of the 1960s, which began when Wolfe profiled Shawn as, "The museum curator, the mummifier, the preserver-in-amber, the smiling embalmer . . . of the *New Yorker*." Wolfe's work has never been printed in the magazine.

21) Answer: C. Apparently, that kind of breakfast food was not conducive to keeping Britney's slim, jailbait figure, so for her next tour she dropped the sugared cereal and instead asked for a bag of Olestra chips.

22) Answer: B. Among the things that Ms. Twain will be carrying to the bus: orange cheese popcorn and Mori Nu silken-style soft tofu.

23) Answer: High-heeled shoes. Blahnik's titanium stiletto "killer" heels taper to a razor-sharp point after 3½ inches. They are so sharp that the designer claims they could easily cut through carpet or another person's foot, making them a dangerous accessory. Another reason for pulling the shoes off the market: They might be mistaken for weapons at airport security scans.

24) Answer: DNA.

25) Answer: Orchestra conductors. "Totally daft" is what British conductor Andrew Davis said of the jacket, which monitors muscle movement through skin sensors. The old method of training involved the conductor standing in front of a mirror and keeping time with the right hand while the left hand signals expression. In addition to the offense of high-tech methods to teach an old school skill, Davis also resented the fabric. He said, "The idea of wearing Lycra is totally appalling to me."

26) Answer: Not seen the play. Matthew Wright wrote in London's *Mirror* that the play *The Dead Monkey* was the worst West End show he'd ever seen. He alleged that only 45 people had attended the Monday night performance, and that the audience had laughed derisively at David Soul. One problem: The theater was closed on Mondays. Soul's lawyer alleged that Wright had sent a free-lance writer to a Thursday-night performance in a more than half-full theater. Soul reportedly received more than $200,000 in damages.

27) Answer: Marlon Brando. Director Frank Oz went to Brando's house and offered him 3 million dollars to play the role of a gay master thief in the 2001 film *The Score*, but when Brando showed up on the set wearing livid makeup and talking with a lisp, Oz tried to steer him toward a more low-key portrayal. Brando responded with typically mumbled profanity and refused to come on the set if Oz was there. Co-star Robert DeNiro ended up directing Brando's scenes, with Oz sending in suggestions from another room.

28) Answer: A. Jakob is a little sensitive about his connection to his iconic father. The Wallflowers first record tanked, and Jakob completely replaced all the other band members for the more successful second record.

29) Answer: B. We are assured by Mr. Richman that the bits of plane fabric in each pen are genuine, even though the plane itself is in the Smithsonian. He says the fabric came from scraps left in the workshop.

30) Answer: A. When you pull the string on Dr. Freud's pillow, it says, "Vy don't you lay down on zee couch?"

31) Answer: Drummer. In the world of rock-and-roll, it's the lead singer and the guitarists who get all the attention *and* most of the groupies. So nobody wants to play the drums; even famous drummers like Phil Collins and Tommy Lee don't drum anymore. Says former Nirvana drummer and current Foo Fighters lead singer Dave Grohl, "Look at the songs they let Ringo sing. 'Yellow Submarine.' If he could have sung 'Let It Be,' then all drummers could have been respected."

32) Answer: *Porky's.*

33) Answer: Kevlar. It's a bulletproof vest. The designer, Galit Levi, says she wants people to know that even in the middle of violence in Israel between Jews and Arabs, life—and fashion—go on. The army-issue flak jacket will, according to the AP, be decorated with diamonds to give it a softer look.

34) Answer: Elvis impersonators. According to Gordon Forbes, a producer of a documentary on Elvis impersonators, only about 150 people imitated the King for either pleasure or money in 1977. Now there are 85,000. That 57,000-percent increase, if it continues, would result in about 3 billion Elvis impersonators in 20 years—about a third of the global population.

35) Answer: Winnie the Pooh. The Canadian Medical Association has released "Pathology in the Hundred Acre Wood"—a tongue-in-cheek psychoanalysis of A. A. Milne's *House on Pooh Corner*. Among the many disturbing revelations in the article is the prognosis for young Roo. "We predict we will someday see a delinquent, jaded, adolescent Roo hanging out late at night—the ground littered with broken bottles of extract of malt and the butts of smoked thistles."

36) Answer: Barbie. Utah artist Tom Forsythe was talking about his series of photographs, titled "Food Chain Barbie." The photos showed the plastic icon of impossible beauty cavorting or otherwise posed with mixers, martini glasses, and in the most famous of the photos, wrapped in tortillas and topped with cheese to create "Enchilada Barbie." Forsythe says his photos show "how society consumes and ingests the ideals expressed in the Barbie doll." Mattel took Forsythe to court claiming copyright infringement—the 65th time the doll's manufacturer has sued an artist for toying with Barbie—but Judge Ronald Lew ruled the photos were a parody and threw Mattel's suit out of court.

37) Answer: Leon Botstein, President of Bard College in New York. Bard was ranked 39th among liberal arts colleges this year by *U. S. News & World Report's* annual college ranking. Mr. Botstein is getting help in his complaint from Amy Graham, a former *U. S. News* employee who oversaw the rankings for 2 years. She writes in *Washington Monthly* magazine that the way the magazine gathers data and ranks colleges doesn't measure the success of graduates, but instead measures things like a school's wealth, reputation, and the amount of alumni giving.

38) Answer: C. Hasbro knew that as soon as they started making the action figures, copycats would go to work. You can't copyright the features of a human face, but you can, it turns out, copyright a scar.

39) Answer: A. In reality, GI Joe's head was created by a sculptor who was paid $600 to create a "good-looking American man." Interestingly, the first African-American GI Joe, which came out a year later, had exactly the same features, dyed brown.

40) Answer: A. "We wouldn't like to name the museum at this time because they may want to keep this under wraps, but we have been approached by another museum for "Dead Dino," "Dinosaur Breath," and "Dinosaur Poo," says Frank Knight of Dale Air Deodorising in Lancastershire, England, discussing dinosaur smells.

41) Answer: Plastic surgeons. The cosmetic surgery industry owes much of its success over the past decade to the popular syndicated TV show. Plastic surgeons say that during the show's heyday in the mid-1990s, potential patients would bring in pictures of *Baywatch* stars to show what they wanted out of their cosmetic surgery. Surgeon Leonard Grossman said, "We were blessed with *Baywatch*. It's like an hour-long plastic-surgery commercial."

42) Answer: Country music. As the Atlanta *Journal and Constitution* put it, country music is in such bad shape, it would make a good country song. Record sales have dropped dramatically partly because, focus groups revealed, most people associate country music with rednecks, white trash, and wife-beating beer drinkers. So, the Country Music Association is unleashing a multimillion-dollar ad campaign centered on the slogan, "Country. Admit it. You love it." Plus, with the prospect of widespread misery, things might be looking up for country. It's the kind of music people listen to when they're dealing with real issues in their lives. And layoffs would be one of them.

43) Answer: The Village People. Hughes was the sextet's mustachioed, leather-clad biker and was working as a toll collector when he answered the ad on a dare. Within 2 years of their first single they were, for a short time, the biggest-selling group in the world. And their biggest hit, "YMCA," is still a sing-along staple at baseball games nationwide. Hughes stayed with the band for years after they fell off the charts. The *Times* of London reported that all but the Indian were later "outed" as heterosexual.

44) Answer: Art. The 2,000 participants were museumgoers, who led researchers to conclude that art "stimulates the erotic senses." The participants all viewed Renaissance, Baroque, and Classical masterpieces before their encounters, and agreed that these were particularly conducive to their romantic moods. Many of those who viewed art with a companion also reported experiencing "an amorous upsurge" even if the art was viewed in a church.

45) Answer: Tossed it in the trash. A janitor at the Eyestorm Gallery took a look at the work and decided that it was just more work for him, which was understandable, given that it really was trash. Hirst had taken used cups, empty beer bottles, and full ashtrays from a gallery party and arranged them into an impromptu installation, instantly valued at 5,000 pounds. The custodian defended his . . . critique . . . telling the *New York Times*, "As soon as I clapped my eyes on it, I sighed because there was so much mess. It didn't look much like art to me. So I cleared it all and dumped it."

46) Answer: Flashing the crowd. Flasher the Clown was kicked out of the Walnut Festival parade because of complaints about his act. Flasher walks around and opens his coat to reveal a small dog peering out of the front of his pants. Flasher, aka Bob Manion, told the *Contra Costa Times* that he's been part of the parade for 30 years and he's not about to change because of a few complaints.

47) Answer: B. Politically, Marston was an advocate of female equality, but psychologically he was more interested in female dominance. In a 1942 interview, he said, "Wonder Woman satisfies the subconscious, elaborately disguised desire of males to be mastered by a woman who loves them."

48) Answer: C. The sorority girls. This brings up a shadowy issue in the history of Wonder Woman. In the original stories, she seemed to get tied up a fair amount. In fact, her one weakness was that she would lose all her power if her wrists were tied together.

49) Answer: B. Zsa Zsa, a refugee from Nazi-occupied Hungary, ended up in Turkey, where she eventually married a Turkish diplomat. But Kemal Attaturk plucked the flower first. She says, "He dazzled me with his sexual prowess and seduced me with his perversion."

50) Answer: Julia Child. Mrs. Child, the original television chef, is wrapping up her long career with a reissue of the book that started it all: *Mastering the Art of French Cooking*, which 40 years ago revealed the wonders of cooking everything in butter. She's moving from her longtime home in Cambridge, Massachusetts, back to California, where she grew up—as you heard—the non-cooking daughter of an upper-class family.

51) Answer: Joan Crawford, who was taking a swipe at longtime screen rival Bette Davis. The two actresses enjoyed a long-lasting feud that began with Crawford's marriage to Davis's leading man from the movie *Dangerous*, Franchot Tone, with whom Davis was rumored to have had an affair. From that point, the battle was on. Joan became known for her ambitious marriages—three movie men and a Pepsi mogul—and Davis as the actress who specialized in a certain role. As Davis put it, "Why am I so good at playing bitches? I think it's because I'm not (one). Maybe that's why Miss Crawford always plays ladies."

52) Answer: Liberace. The performer who was perhaps the greatest diva of them all commented on Barbra Streisand, who opened for him at the Riviera Hotel in Las Vegas in 1963. For some reason, Barbra thought that muted brown and gray gowns would work well to open for the ever-understated Liberace. It didn't. To salvage her performance, he rearranged the program so that he would announce her as a special discovery in the middle of his act, promising the audience that he'd return with their favorite numbers just as soon as she was done singing. She was also made to wear a gold dress with some showy earrings.

53) Answer: Bob Dylan. Dylan told the *Los Angeles Times* that he dislikes contemporary music so much that if he were coming of age today, he'd turn to mathematics or architecture instead. Dylan said, "I know there are groups at the top of the charts that are hailed as saviors of rock and roll and all that, but they are amateurs. They don't know where the music comes from." He also said that he doesn't mind when people respond negatively to his own music saying, "Miles Davis has been booed, Hank Williams was booed, Stravinsky was booed."

54) Answer: C. It was an understandable mistake since the marriage lasted only 6 months. In marriage, the Gabors were prolific: Zsa Zsa ended up with nine husbands, Eva, only five.

55) Answer: A. Stalin World. The park, opened by a Lithuanian mushroom magnate who already has the world's largest collection of Soviet-era statues, features fake guard towers and a cafeteria serving Soviet delicacies like fish head soup and gruel.

Foreign News

1) Answer: A. As anyone who's seen *Mary Poppins* knows, a favorite thing to do in London is buy a packet of birdseed from the kindly old peddler and feed the pigeons, "tuppence a bag." But no more. The last birdseed seller was paid to go out of business to decrease the pigeon population in Trafalgar Square.

2) Answer: Drunk.

3) Answer: The U. S. Embassy. The unidentified gullible Romanian bought part of the embassy from Traian Balan Toderascu, who, according to police, used an accomplice to steal the deed from the city archives. They then forged the other papers they needed. No word on what the buyer thought when he visited the property and encountered dozens of American officials.

4) Answer: Nudity. Parents at Sawtell Primary School in North Coast, Australia, have released a calendar with photos of 12 local businessmen in the buff. Some are parents; some aren't. They're trying to raise enough money to pay for a covered lunch area at the school. One of the parents said the calendars are selling well ". . . especially amongst the elderly community. I have taken a lot up to the retirement home," she said.

5) Answer: Moving furniture. John Turner filed for divorce because his wife moved furniture obsessively around their home, every day of their life together. Mrs. Turner says, "Moving furniture about was just something I did and I always will do. I suppose everybody has their little obsession."

6) Answer: Nails. Fire broke out on the roof of a building in Hong Kong's central district, but the women at Fingertrix salon said they would not be evacuated until their nails were perfect. Salon owner Rebecca Lee told Reuters, "We took the risk because we wanted to get the job done." The three staffers and two customers left an hour later, after the acrylic nails were fabulous and after the fire had been extinguished.

7) Answer: Ad. Scientists at England's Rutherford Appleton Laboratory have created an advertisement so small, you can fit it around the knee of a bee. The ad is about the width of a human hair and simply reads "GuinnessWorld Record.com." While an ad not visible to the naked eye may not be the best way to get the word out, it has given the folks at Guinness bragging rights.

8) Answer: Lard—the other off-white nougat. Ukrainians are lining up to get the candy bars made by a local confectioner. The bars are exactly what you would think—a stick of fat covered in chocolate. They are being sold as a light-hearted joke among Ukrainians, who traditionally enjoy salted pork fat as an ac-companiment to vodka and pickles.

9) Answer: Brothels. There are 900 legal brothels in Australia that receive an estimated 12 million visits per year—or two for every Aussie male. According to the National Tax and Accountants' Association, the gift of a brothel visit is tax deductible to the employer, so it's become a popular year-end bonus. "We don't think it's appropriate for the Christmas season," said John Barridge from the Australian Family Association. "Why can't we stick to the old ways of a bottle of whiskey or a free pass to a restaurant?"

10) Answer: A tin of sauerkraut. The unnamed 71-year-old employee was busy stacking cans of pickled cabbage when the two masked robbers threatened a female shop assistant with a pistol. With kraut in hand, the hero approached the villains, heaving a can and hitting the armed man in the head. Startled, the robbers left without a cent.

11) Answer: Women's panties. One-hundred-and-forty pairs of multicolored panties were recently mailed to the military's top brass by an anonymous critic or critics. The military is insulted because they think it means they're weak. Venezuelan feminists are insulted because the military thinks that women's un-derwear implies weakness.

12) Answer: Cell phones. According to the food trade magazine *The Grocer*, the fall in British chocolate sales from $3.9 to $3.7 billion is directly connected to the fact that the country's youth are investing their tuppence in Nokia over nougat. Said *The Grocer's* Simon Mowbray, "Children are walking into stores and instead of buying a Mars bar they are scrabbling together enough change to buy a £4 phone card so they can keep using their mobiles."

13) Answer: Starting a fire beneath it. The 78-year-old man from a cold Bavarian village was having a hard time starting his car, so to warm it up he ignited a pile of paper towels in a metal box and placed the box beneath the engine. The vehicle quickly caught fire and was destroyed. The man, presumably still stupid, was not injured.

14) Answer: Bee. The buzzing little fella was just looking for a warm place to live—and found it inside the circuit board of a rail-switching station outside Tokyo. The bee jammed the switch, forcing the trains to stop. A spokesperson for the Japan Railway said that although bees look for warm places to hide during cool weather, he had never heard of one stopping the trains, though he did remember a turtle that got stuck between the switchboard rails once.

15) Answer: It would ruin her hair. The 53-year-old transsexual magician who performs as Fay Presto got off with a warning when she told the judge she was on her way to a gig at Marco Pierre White's Criterion restaurant. No word on whether the judge was a patron, an adoring fan, or just understood the importance of good hair.

16) Answer: Had no idea where he was going. Passengers like Peter Hart were understandably irate. He said, "I've heard all sorts of excuses, but how do you lose your way on the train? It's bananas."

17) Answer: Cursed by gypsies. The Bishop of Oxford went to the New Kassam stadium, sprinkled holy water over the center circle, and prayed for the wicked spirit to be cast out. The stadium was built on a field where gypsies used to park their caravans. They cursed the team upon their eviction. The chairman of Oxford United said he hopes the blessing will help the team out of its slump. "Now the manager can't blame the gypsies if we don't start winning more matches."

18) Answer: Climbing a tree and throwing bananas. Firefighters were called to the scene and brought with them an airbag and a psychologist. The bag was placed under the tree and the shrink was hoisted up the tree in a bucket. The firefighters are planning on billing the tree climber for their services—at least $1,000. No word on what the psychologist charges for tree calls.

19) Answer: Stork. Saturn the Stork crash-landed in Burundi, prompting the villagers who found him to turn him in to the police. Apparently, they noticed the satellite-tracking collar around his neck and became suspicious. The police took Saturn into custody and inspected the tracking device, which revealed the name of Les Underhill. He's a University of Cape Town professor who studies migratory bird patterns. Underhill admitted that the device looks "pretty Space Age."

20) Answer: Popcorn tubs.

21) Answer: Go disco dancing. Doctors at Dortmund University wanted the man to go home, and took him to court to force him to leave. But the unnamed 95-year old man wouldn't leave until he was assured that he could freestyle on the dance floor. The court gave the man 2 weeks to leave.

22) Answer: Smell. Having studied the United Kingdom, British nutritionist Kevin Gould says he can tell where a person is from by their body odor. For example, if you smell goatish, you are most likely from Scotland. Likewise, if you give off an aroma of rotten eggs, you are most likely from Newcastle or Manchester. According to Mr. Gould, this all has to do with regional diets. If you wash down your haggis with whiskey, you'll smell like a goat, and if you eat a lot of fish, as they do in Essex, you'll smell fishy.

23) Answer: Pimple. Two nurses at a hospital in Cardiff, South Wales, were suspended after a colleague caught them squeezing the pimples of an unconscious patient. The incident was immediately reported to the hospital's general manager, who began an investigation. After concluding that no harm was done, the nurses returned to work, though stripped of their tweezers.

24) Answer: Men. In an effort to cut down on street crime and domestic abuse, Bogotá, Colombia, Mayor Anatanas Mockus instituted the "Night Without Men." Described as the Lilith Fair meets the running of the bulls, wild women filled the streets for one glorious night of dancing, discounted drinks, and male strippers. A police force of 1,500 women was on hand to bust any men loitering without the mandatory safe-conduct passes, or Passports of Love, as they came to be known. Crime was down that night by 25 percent.

25) Answer: Quit smoking.

26) Answer: Prime Minister Tony Blair's vacation. "I couldn't believe it when I saw Tony Blair looking back at me," said David Devlin of Glasgow. "At first I didn't recognize him, as he was holding his baby son in front of his face. But in the next shot, it was obvious." Devlin called the film processor who instructed him to return the photos. A spokeswoman for the Blairs said that the Prime Minister is grateful to Devlin for returning them.

27) Answer: Bras. The 40 women brought the Prince nearly $1½ million dollars they raised for breast cancer charities. "I was so interested to see the sheer inventiveness when you came to the gate," said the Prince as he smilingly received the half-naked women at his estate. Charity organizer Nina Barough said she wanted to give him a hug, but unfortunately, her silver cone-shaped bra with its lacy rose-patterned trim was too intrusive.

28) Answer: Pedestrian. The word "pedestrian" is, it seems, a serious turn off, said Ben Plowden, director of the Pedestrian Society. People are unhappy because of its negative associations. "The group is as much about stopping as walking, having time and space to daydream, sit on a bench, chat to your neighbor or snog your girlfriend," said Plowden. The new, sassier name: "Living Streets."

29) Answer: Lost. "Lost is a tiny village and it's quite difficult to find at the best of times," said Aberdeenshire tourist board spokeswoman Beverly Tricker. "Now that someone has taken the signpost, people are getting even more lost. We are appealing for Lost to be found."

30) Answer: Grumpy. The Quebec Superior Court upheld the rights of a man who disinherited his family and left all his money to a charity that helps sick children. Family members testified that the man's profound grumpiness was a sign of his dementia, but the judge honored the will.

31) Answer: C. Francis Galton had an intriguing and eccentric interest in numbers. The kind of observation he liked best was numerical, and this propensity led him to establish a beauty map of Britain, by noting the frequency of which he saw attractive women in various towns.

32) Answer: Diseases. The Finns are tired of having diseases named after them. Researchers who discover a disease get to name it and they often name it after the region where it's most prominent. But doctors meeting at the World Medical Association conference in Paris got an earful from Finns tired of new diseases being named after places in their homeland—for example there is Salla disease, Pogosta disease, and Kumlinge disease, all named after areas of Finland.

33) Answer: Beer. Irish eyes were smiling as workers at the Guinness plant scheduled to close in Dundalk, Ireland, voted to receive their severance package in beer. Of course, they also received some cash, health insurance benefits, even scholarships for their children. But some senior employees will get free beer for 10 years. Said Guinness spokesman Pat Berry, "It is a tradition within the industry that employees get a beer allowance, amounting to around two bottles a day."

34) Answer: Godzilla. Raging through the world on a rampage of destruction—it's the king of the lunchmeats, Godzilla. A Japanese toy company is introducing Godzilla meat in a can. For about $5, you can buy a decorative can of Godzilla meat, which tastes eerily similar to corned beef. A company spokesman says people who eat it will become powerful like Popeye and his can of spinach.

35) Answer: Flirting. The Italian Gestalt Institute reported that 7 out of 10 Italians, men and women, say that flirting with coworkers makes for a more relaxed, pleasant work environment. Not only that, but they say getting a little erotic buzz on the side helps them feel more confident and relaxed when they get home. But apparently there are limits. Twenty percent of those asked admit that their flirtatious relationships developed into "serious passion," leaving them feeling stressed, depressed, and unable to sleep.

36) Answer: The Queen.

37) Answer: Fax. Prison officials on the island of Corsica received an official-looking fax that said to release the prisoners. The fax was signed by the magistrate investigating the prisoners on charges of extortion and illegal possession of firearms. The jailers opened the doors and waved goodbye, but they bothered neither to check the number from which the fax was sent nor to contact the judge to see if the order was genuine.

38) Answer: Tasty in soup. According to Valleybrook Gardens' general manager, Michel Binoit, the label on the perennials should have read, "All parts of this plant are toxic," but as a practical joke, an employee changed it to, "All parts of this plant are tasty in soup." Apparently, the employee thought the prank would be caught by a horticulturalist before any damage was done.

39) Answer: Casting spells on them. High Priest Kevin Carlyon of the British Coven of White Witches wanted to protect the beast from the pesky researchers, so he cast a spell on their boat. Apparently, the Swedes weren't as afraid as they were annoyed. Said one scientist, "I'm trying to be as scientific as possible while he casts his mumbo-jumbo spells. If he shows his face down here again, we'll throw him in the lake."

40) Answer: Banished into space. Makiko Tanaka, sort of like the Bob Dornan of Japan, only she's popular and well-liked, was discussing a former prime minister who appears to making a comeback from political disgrace. Tanaka said, "We should assign such former prime ministers, who are far from humble, to work abroad. If they cannot manage that, we should strap them to satellites."

41) Answer: Zipper. As the *Sun* tabloid put it, "Flashing Was a Dodgy Zip." Sergeant Andrew Chatfield says he wasn't actually flashing the four elderly women at a retirement home—he just had a faulty zipper. Two zipper experts took the stand at his trial to debate whether the police officer's corduroys could have popped open without help. Chatfield says it happened to him several times and that the incidents have increased with his weight.

42) Answer: The Virgin Mary. Customs officials stopped the Colombian citizens after their return flight from Spain. According to the travelers, the sacred

Virgin appeared before them with oodles of greenbacks. Regardless of its origin, it is illegal to bring more than $10,000 in cash into Colombia without declaring it. The adult members of the group were arrested. The Blessed Mother could not be found for comment.

43) Answer: Women's soccer match.

44) Answer: His wife. The missus was there looking for employment. Apparently, much like in the classic story "The Gift of the Magi," both husband and wife had kept their extracurricular activities secret from one another. No word from the police on what either party was using as a defense.

45) Answer: Play golf. In order to play on one of Germany's precious golf courses, you must first take a test of your golf skills, play a round under a maximum score, and also pass a written quiz on the rules. This is to protect the courses, according to the defenders of the system. Among the questions asked on the test: Is it all right to wear sneakers on the golf course? The answer: no.

46) Answer: Common. The Palace released photos of William mingling with the locals and doing chores while traveling in Chile. But Prince Phillip says this sort of thing just isn't done. He told American reporters, "The more accessible you become, the more ordinary you become."

47) Answer: Keijo Kopra, a very angry man in Finland complaining bitterly after he had been fined $47,000 for speeding. In Finland, in what the government says is an old Nordic tradition, traffic fines are based on a person's ability to pay. If you're pulled over doing 60 in Helsinki, the traffic cop will punch your ID into his cell phone and instantly receive on his screen your monthly income and an appropriate fine. Kopra was originally fined $14,000 for going 14 MPH over the speed limit. He challenged it in court, but the judge got mad and eventually more than tripled it.

48) Answer: Itching powder. According to documents released by Kew Public Records Office, itching powder was one of a number of "special devices" available to agents. One British spy manual from the period suggests infiltrating a German brothel and putting the powder inside the prophylactics. Spies were

also equipped with exploding bottles of Chianti and bombs disguised as lumps of coal and rats. The rat explosives, although discovered, scored an unexpected success when the occupation authorities in France wasted valuable time searching hundreds of rats for more explosives.

49) Answer: Vacuum cleaner. The gentleman was choking on a piece of *mochi*, a kind of glutinous rice traditionally eaten on New Years and often a danger to the very young and the elderly. Despite the positive result of the vacuum cleaner application, doctors advise against using vacuum cleaners for any kind of emergency medical procedure.

50) Answer: Coconuts. Officials on the Solomons estimate that at least one person a day is being hit in the noggin by a falling coconut. Sure, it sounds funny, but coconuts weigh about 8 pounds apiece, so they present a definite health danger. One local doctor says he's treated at least 130 people for coconut-related injuries.

51) Answer: Pregnant. Eight women have become pregnant after sitting in a certain chair at the Gala Bingo Hall—a quarter of the workforce. Helen Hutt, an official at the Hall, said that some customers are asking to sit on the chair, believing it's somehow lucky.

52) Answer: Saddam Hussein. Intelligence analysts believe that the anonymously authored Arabic novel *Zabibah and the King* was either written by Hussein himself or written by others under his close supervision. It describes the relationship between an all-powerful king and a peasant girl who adores him. As for Mr. Bowser, whose art was used without permission, he doesn't expect to get anything from the famously homicidal military dictator. He says, "There is surely a very long list of people with more significant grievances than I have against Saddam Hussein."

53) Answer: The Israeli Knesset. The Knesset has long been known for its spirited discussions, but Ethics Committee Chair Colette Avital got fed up, so she circulated a list of insulting terms with the suggestion that lawmakers be fined for using them. Her colleagues objected, however, noting that the Knesset is not a manners school, and further suggesting that Ms. Avital is an idiotic, blood-drinking swamp fly.

54) Answer: Yoga. The clergy flipped over the Slovakian government's recent proposal to teach yoga in schools. "Yoga is not gymnastics," said Protestant bishop Ivan Osusky, claiming the practice led to individualism and Hinduism. Roman Catholic bishops concurred, identifying the practice as a gateway to atheism. Bishop Osusky went on to say, "There are risks associated with foreign influences. Thank God we are not America. Too much tolerance is harmful."

55) Answer: Court jester. The island nation's legislative assembly is investigating the case of Jesse Bogdonoff, a North Carolina native, who impressed King Taufa' Ahau Tupou by successfully investing the kingdom's money, prompting the King to name Bogdonoff Tonga's Court Jester. But the money disappeared. Said one Tongan minister, "It looks like the money's gone and it looks like we are the laughingstock of the world again." Lawsuits are in the works.

56) Answer: Squirrels. Madden thought he had come up with the perfect bird-feeding hat—headwear fitted with a feeding tray full of tasty nuts to tempt the birds for close-up viewing. But on his first test run in the woods, Madden was hit by a squirrel that took a leap at him from the top of a tree. The squirrel knocked Madden to the ground, causing minor injuries and a hasty return to the drawing board.

57) Answer: Potato. Some 2,000 people had to be evacuated during a performance by the San Francisco Ballet when a potato exploded inside a backstage microwave, setting off fire alarms. Trevor Sumner from the London fire service said, "It's quite odd because our lads often microwave their baked potatoes and we've never had this happen."

58) Answer: Broke wind. The Yard's internal discipline body investigated eight officers over allegations that one broke wind during a drug bust in Chingford, Essex. Why did this act require the attention of internal affairs? It wasn't the act of wind breaking. The charge of "incivility" resulted from the fact that the officer did not apologize afterward.

59) Answer: B. Chick sexer. It wasn't until the 1920s when Japanese chicken growers developed a reliable way to examine the pertinent "equipment" on newly hatched chicks. The Japanese became the best chick sexers in the world, but new chicken breeds are easier to sex and highly skilled workers are no longer necessary.

60) Answer: Glue. A driver on an Italian roadway was stuck in traffic for hours after a truck loaded with extra-strength construction glue crashed in front of his car. When he got out of his vehicle, he stepped into the adhesive and was glued there for the better part of the day. He told his rescuers that being glued to the road gave him an opportunity "to enjoy the landscape."

61) Answer: Ghost. Tony Cornell, a British expert on the occult, says cell phones are chasing away ghosts. He claims ghost sightings have dropped significantly since the introduction of cell phones years ago. Mr. Cornell told London's *Express* newspaper that haunted tourist attractions could be threatened if the popularity of cell phones continues to grow.

Politics

1) Answer: C. "In Chicago, we have 750,000 households we collect from. Basically, we go in and pick up half-empty, empty, or full. If there was some way we could take advantage of this, we would certainly be interested in looking at it, but I'm just wondering if the city of Barcelona has alleys or if it's all curbside. All these things factor into the efficiency and economics of garbage collection," says Ray Padvoiskis, spokesman for the Chicago Department of Streets and Sanitation discussing the Barcelona microchip litter bin project.

2) Answer: Frogs. Caribbean tree frogs, to be precise. Apparently, this breed of tree frog can be stimulated to death.

3) Answer: Shepherds.

4) Answer: Traffic accidents.

5) Answer: Parking. Scott Eshleman never denied that he'd been drinking the night he was arrested after police found him asleep in his Chevy Blazer, but there was no evidence he actually drove the car in his drunken state. His girlfriend testified that she drove the car to its location and left Eshleman to sleep off his partying. The judge convicted him nonetheless, but the appeals court overturned the conviction, saying that the judge had, in effect, created a new crime: "parked while intoxicated."

6) Answer: Relieved herself in a trashcan. Irene Smith was trying to hold up debate on a redistricting plan when nature called. Alderman President James Shrewsbury ruled if Smith left the floor, she yielded the floor, so aides surrounded her with a tablecloth and a quilt, and she appeared to use a wastebasket to answer nature's call. Smith said, "What I did behind that tablecloth is my business." A spokesman for St. Louis Mayor Francis Slay had a different take on the incident. He said, "The people in Missouri must think we're a bunch of morons."

7) Answer: B. Despite the kindness of the Capitol staff toward his portrait, the Senate itself voted to condemn him. He died believing he would be vindicated by history, but he was wrong.

8) Answer: The *Chicago Times*. So wrote the *Chicago Times* about a speech by one of our better-known presidents—Abraham Lincoln's Gettysburg Address. Apparently, Lincoln's crisp writing and speaking was not the fashion of the time and was considered too lowbrow to befit the stature of a President. The organizers of the event must have shared this opinion of Lincoln's elocutionary prowess, since the featured speaker of the day was Edward Everett, whose 1,500 hundred flowery, Ciceronian sentences by far overshadowed Lincoln's mere 268 words. Lincoln himself didn't think too highly of his performance that day, and he confided to Everett, "I failed: I failed, and that is about all that can be said about it."

9) Answer: Hands. Sometimes, the habits of the white man would strike Indians as so comical they just had to imitate them for a laugh. White settlers must have been a bit perturbed to see two Indians approach one another, shake hands, and then collapse on the ground laughing. Native Americans were also shocked to find that white parents would grab their children by the ears to discipline them, which inspired Indians to occasionally refer to white people as Flop Ears.

10) Answer: C. "I have several bills that I have pre-found. One in particular has to do with people who come to the door naked," says Georgia State Representative Dorothy Pelote.

11) Answer: Cab drivers. The Port Commission may require stricter grooming rules requiring cabbies to be "free of offensive body odor" and to wear clean clothes and socks.

12) Answer: Hot babe looking for fun.

13) Answer: B. Roosevelt and the Republican Senator started yelling at each other, after which the crowd quickly divided into two factions, and everybody fled the scene soon after the turtle soup course was served.

14) Answer: The Weather Channel. According to Fox News, the Huntsville office of the National Weather Service has five employees but no real responsibilities or equipment. So, they monitor other people's weather reports on a computer and watch a muted TV tuned to the Weather Channel.

15) Answer: Pants or pantsuits.

16) Answer: Wave a flag. In the search for low-cost pedestrian protection, the Berkeley City Council decided to place brightly colored flags at either end of each crosswalk. The flags may be removed from their holders and waved prominently to alert passing automobiles. When asked about the humiliation factor of waving a flag in public, Polly Armstrong, who proposed the idea to the council, said, "I think some people will feel silly, but you know, it's better than feeling dead."

17) Answer: Sore losers. Mayor Daniel Stewart says he's tired of dealing with people who think their backlit nativity scene is a real work of art, so no more contest. In previous years, a committee awarded certificates naming several homes as "best decorated." One homeowner admitted he complained after spending 2 days decorating his house only to lose to a guy who bought a plastic light-up Santa.

18) Answer: Dead lawyer joke. The ad, supposed to encourage people to drive more safely, has a folksy fellow saying, "A car full of lawyers turned over right in front of Old Man Jenkins' place. He comes out and buries them all. The sheriff asked Old Man Jenkins, 'You sure they were all dead?' 'Well,' says Jenkins, 'Some said they weren't, but you know how them lawyers lie.'"

19) Answer: Nothing. The council voted unanimously to suspend the mayor's pay of $766 a month because, "He is pretty much not doing anything." For his part, Bozardt responded that he had very good excuses for not attending the council meetings he missed, and that he did prepare a budget, but nobody called him back. Or something.

20) Answer: Related to a president. *Family Tree* editor Susan Wenner says that New Englanders have the greatest chance of a presidential branch in their tree. As for the rest of us, we're probably related to 10th President John Tyler who sired 15 children. As for the more impressive high-profile presidents, it is unlikely that anyone is descended from George Washington, since experts believe he was sterile.

21) Answer: Drunk. Wichita Falls, Texas, Mayor Jerry Lueck learned a valuable lesson while visiting his town's sister city, Fuerstenfeldbruck, Germany—don't drink and then try to say, "The Burgermeister of Fuerstenfeldbruck." According to the Dallas morning news, Mayor Lueck enjoyed a little too much of the local brew and reportedly referred to his host as the "Boogermeister" or "Burgermaster." The mayor, who also snored audibly through government and military discussions, remains unrepentant, saying, "At no time did I ever make a fool of Wichita Falls."

22) Answer: Mayor. Eighteen-year-old Jeffrey Dunkel was elected mayor of Mount Carbon, Pennsylvania, population 100. While researching local government for a class project, young Mr. Dunkel was politely admonished that if he could do a better job he should prove it. So he ran for mayor unopposed, and won. A unique system of checks and balances is in place for the teenage mayor— his mother was elected to the city council.

23) Answer: A. In 1970, Nixon and Agnew were accused of using a "Southern strategy" to get white support in Southern states during the midterm elections. So Nixon came out to play various songs while Agnew kept interrupting by playing "Dixie." The two ended with a rousing version of "God Bless America."

24) Answer: A. "Gaugin reported to the police that Van Gogh was lying in bed bleeding to death, and in fact it did look like he was bleeding to death. Nobody assumed that he might have had anything to do with it," says Julie Penzel, translator of the Vincent Van Gogh/Paul Gaugin article.

25) Answer: Food. Healthy Choice entrees, to be exact. Oklahoman Keith Griffith was delighted to find that somebody had sent him a package of frozen chicken on a bed of noodles via certified mail, but inside the box was a statement that he owed $9,000 in child support and had 15 days to pay up. Why the entrees? Apparently, the Oklahoma officials found that people often avoid certified letters and that people are more likely to sign for a package, thinking it's a gift.

26) Answer: Each other. At least two dozen Bush staffers have gotten married or coupled up in some fashion. And, according to Department of Justice official Mindy Tucker, the President himself sometimes micromanages the matchmaking. She told the *Washington Post*, "This is definitely a policy priority from the top."

27) Answer: Bill Clinton. Mr. Clinton was playing a round of golf at Rudding Park in Harrogate, North Yorkshire, when he stumbled upon a wedding reception at a nearby hotel. He gamely chatted with the attendees and had his picture taken with the bride and groom. Said the bride's father, "He didn't interfere at all—he lifted the day."

28) Answer: The dead. In response to a scandalous incident in which a funeral home transported some clients, as it were, in the back of a pickup truck, the North Carolina senate amended some regulations governing funeral homes and embalmers. While they were at it, they made sure to add that, "Using profanity, indecent or obscene language in the presence of a dead human body" could result in the revocation of a funeral home's license.

29) Answer: Candy. A Hershey bar to be exact, with an expiration date of 1941. Admiral Byrd took the Army-commissioned bar on his third trip to the South Pole in 1939. Hershey developed the chocolate bar as a high-energy ration for the U. S. Army. One possible reason Admiral Byrd buried his candy may have been the Army's requirement that it taste "just a little better than a boiled potato" so that soldiers wouldn't binge.

30) Answer: B. In addition to giving the President the last word, the club also maintains the tradition of never depicting the sitting President in one of its skits. However, former presidents or candidates are fair game.

31) Answer: Toilets. According to the *Los Angeles Times*, the seven officials spent taxpayer money to go to Europe for 6 days and examine public privies. City Comptroller Laura Chick told the *Times*: "I've been there and I could have told them how the toilets work. My God, pick up the phone and call the Mayor of Paris and London and ask what you need to know."

32) Answer: Just one piece of Halloween candy. According to a survey conducted by AMC-TV, Republicans are more likely to give out one piece of candy per trick-or-treater, while Democrats give out handfuls.

33) Answer: Babes. Here's an excerpt from a White House memo from 1971: "In seating at State Dinners, the President feels that Henry should not always be put next to the most glamorous woman present. He should be put by an intelligent and interesting dinner partner and we should shift from the practice of putting him by the best-looking one. It's starting to cause unfavorable talk that serves no useful purpose."

34) Answer: C. "First of all, it's all about the peanut butter. The main flavor you get is the peanut butter and then the jelly kicks in. They look like they're layered. Yes, there's a layer of peanut butter on both sides of the jelly. That's patentable, huh?" says Michael Dixon, our willing UnCrustables taster from Louisville, Kentucky.

35) Answer: A. The article was written by former U. S. Ambassador to Moscow Joseph Davies, the subject of the infamous wartime movie *Mission to Moscow*, which was the center of the first postwar investigations of Communists in Hollywood.

36) Answer: Edward Kennedy. He wore number 88 for the Harvard Crimson football team from 1954 to 1956 and must have had talent. Not to mention the potential for off-the-field antics.

37) Answer: We/us/Americans. From the beginning of our nation's history, many people thought that "United States of America" was an unsatisfactory name for a country, especially since it lacked a proper adjectival form. "United-Statesian" is too awkward and "American" isn't precise enough since it covers citizens of other countries on the continent as well. The alternatives to America that were considered included Columbia, Appalachia, Alleghenia, and Freedonia (or Fredonia), which would be home to the Freeds (or Fredes).

38) Answer: Doodling or drawing cartoons. Judge Frederick Arnold allowed police to draw happy or frowny faces on traffic tickets to describe a driver's attitude at the time of the citation. The state supreme court said the doodles were illegal and found Judge Arnold guilty of willful misconduct.

39) Answer: Elvis Presley. The letter was sent by Elvis Presley, who was asking for credentials to become a federal agent in order to selflessly help his country. To show his credentials, he added, "The Drug Culture, the Hippie Elements, the S. D. S., Black Panthers, etc do not consider me as their enemy or as they call it the Establishment. I was nominated this coming year as one of America's Ten Most Outstanding Young Men." To butter up the president, Elvis adds in a P. S., "I believe that you Sir were one of the Top Ten Outstanding Men of America also." He also included a gift of a Colt .45 pistol. A meeting did take place and the famous photograph of the King and Nixon shaking hands is now the single most requested image from the National Archives.

40) Answer: Republican presidential nominee Rutherford B. Hayes in a letter to his wife. Wheeler was William A. Wheeler the vice-presidential nominee who was a fairly anonymous congressman. His main claim to fame was that he once protested a raise in salary by giving his money back to the government. Because Hayes was from Ohio, the Republican convention of 1876 needed a candidate from New York to run with him in order to gain the votes of that important state. The delegates didn't really care who it was since it was only the vice-presidency. The New York delegates began joking and finally said, "Let's give it to Wheeler!"

41) Answer: Hair. Cheyenne warriors prepared for battle by putting on their best clothes, painting themselves, and rebraiding their hair. If they didn't have time to finish any of these preparations, they would run away. And the Crow loved long hair, gumming horsetail extensions into their hair to increase length. In the 1830s, they had a chief called Long Hair whose hair was 11 feet, 6 inches long. White travelers would frequently stop to measure Chief Long Hair's hair.

42) Answer: B. In addition to antiheroes like Mao and Ho Chi Minh, the cards featured frightening scenarios of a fictional Olga and Ivan who answer a knock at the door and are told where to work, where to live, and what subjects they must master at school.

Science

1) Answer: B. "Putting a number on the crunchiness of something eliminates the subjectivity of human testers. Of course, that means that those people will be out of their jobs or will have to retrain as crunch meter operators," says Hame Watsmen, who wrote about the crunch meter in *New Scientist* magazine.

2) Answer: Shirt. Japan-based Fuji Spinning Company has developed a vitamin C-enriched T-shirt called V-Up. The shirt is made from fibers that contain a chemical called pro-vitamin that leaches into the skin, giving the wearer the equivalent of two lemons worth of vitamins. The company is in the process of designing shirts loaded with other vitamins and is working on a design for enriched underwear.

3) Answer: Australian. DNA tests on Mungo Man, a 60,000-year-old Australian skeleton, reveal that our most modern ancestors may have come from Australia. This discovery adds weight to the theory that humans arose simultaneously from various locations, as opposed to the "Out of Africa" theory, which posits that all human life sprang from that continent.

4) Answer: Water. A study released by the University of Bristol has determined that drinking water when you're not thirsty increases human idiocy. Researchers testing 60 people discovered a 15-percent drop in mental ability of those who drank a cold glass of water when they weren't thirsty. Psychologist Peter Rogers blames the lapse on the temperature of the water and the body's need to "deal with the local cooling effect in the gut."

5) Answer: C. The prefix "arachi" refers to the sticky oil found in nuts and nut butters.

6) Answer: A. "So he came up with the ingenious idea of taking a hair dryer, cutting off the cord, wrapping it up in tape, and when traffic was coming too fast, he'd just point it at them and it just slows them down," says John DeWitt, chairman of the Escambia County School Board.

7) Answer: E-mail. That was engineer Ray Tomlinson talking to Reuters about e-mail, something he invented 30 years ago that has become absolutely ubiquitous. In 1971, Tomlinson invented a way to send a message to any computer connected to a central network. He also invented the use of the @ sign to create Internet addresses.

8) Answer: Kissing. A California dentist got his name in the paper with the news that kissing can cause cavities. Dr. Laurence Rifkin made the announcement that "the relationship between sharing food and kissing may pass on bacteria that can cause decay." As a result of the news, a new rejection phrase has been added to the American dating vernacular: "It's not you, I'm just thinking about my teeth."

9) Answer: Fat. A team of researchers at UCLA and the University of Pittsburgh have taken human fat removed by liposuction and turned it into bone, cartilage, and muscle. The scientists isolated stem cells, which are immature cells that can be manipulated into transforming into specific types of tissue. Researchers are optimistic that in the near future they will be able to use a patient's own fat to repair tissue and treat disease.

10) Answer: Orgasms. Pain specialist Dr. Stuart Meloy was testing the device for back pain on a patient recovering from multiple back surgeries when she let out a moan and told the doctor, "You're going to have to teach my husband how to do that." Apparently, the device needs to be placed very precisely to target the specific nerve bundles causing a patient's discomfort, so a slight adjustment can cause, well, other sensations.

11) Answer: Everywhere. We're talking about the "Universal Constant," a controversial theory suggested by Einstein that posited the existence of a mysterious force that counteracted the effects of gravity, forcing all things in the universe apart. Even Einstein came to think the idea was ridiculous, but study of photos of a distant supernova taken by the Hubble Space Telescope several years ago have proven the existence of this force. This means, among other things, that the universe will not collapse once again for another Big Bang, as was previously thought, but will continue expanding and growing dimmer until it finally dies out.

12) Answer: C. "There's a modem inside the actual toaster so it's connected to a phone line and then you dial up the server. The server recognizes where you are in the country and passes back the weather forecast for your local area," according to Robin Southgate, inventor of the Weather Toaster.

13) Answer: A. The first PEZ product was an Altoid-like mint sold as an aid to quit smoking. It was a disaster when introduced in the United States in the 1950s. Then, some genius had the idea of putting them in little spring-loaded dispensers with heads, and a phenomenon was born.

14) Answer: C. A Florida perfume company has signed a deal to make and distribute PEZ scents. The company says it's not looking at candy scents, but "quality fragrances you'd be proud to wear."

15) Answer: Tick. Scientists in New Jersey believe they have found the world's oldest tick. The 90 million-year-old tick was found buried in a vacant lot in Sayreville, embedded in amber.

16) Answer: Neanderthal. Researchers in England say that "the ginger gene," which causes red hair, fair skin, and freckles may be a legacy from our extinct ancient cousins, the Neanderthals. Homo sapiens came to Europe from Africa about 50,000 years ago, but the red-hair gene is at least 100,000 years old, meaning it might have come from the more ancient Neanderthals.

17) Answer: A. We have no idea what one could fear in a chin, but we remind you that the whole point is that these fears are irrational.

18) Answer: C. The Walloons speak Walloon, a romance language similar to French, and as far as we know, they've never hurt anybody, but again, the whole point is that these fears are irrational.

19) Answer: B. "If the system notices through its sensors that the driver is falling asleep, it will ask if the driver would like to spend the night in a hotel or tell a joke because we know that jokes have great entertainment value and would keep people awake," says Valdek Zedrozny of IBM's T. J. Watson Research Laboratory.

20) Answer: Jet lag. Globetrotters take note, jet lag will shrink your brain. Scientists at the University of Bristol studied the effects of jet lag on 20 flight attendants. Those who had little time between flights that crossed multiple time zones suffered lapses in short-term memory. An MRI scan confirmed that their brains were shrinking, specifically the right temporal lobe of the brain, the area that affects the memory.

21) Answer. Scots. According to Oxford University's *Human Reproduction* magazine, Scottish men are the most sexually potent in Europe. Sure, the French are suave, and the Italians dark and seductive, but it's the Scottish men who are delivering the goods these days. Concern that sperm levels were falling lead scientists to study 1,000 men from different European cities. The men of Edinburgh had the most motile sperm, meaning most likely to reach and fertilize the egg.

22) Answer: Blind. You can now add french fries and Nutter Butters to the list of things to avoid if you want to keep your sight. A study by the Massachusetts Eye and Ear Infirmary found that foods high in vegetable, monounsaturated and polyunsaturated fats—things like cookies, potato chips, store-made cakes—can increase your risk of macular degeneration, which is the leading cause of vision loss in adults over 50. To avoid this cruel fate, the study recommends eating lots of leafy greens and fish.

23) Answer: C. One typical ad read, "One husband for sale. Balding, often cranky, stomach requiring considerable attention."

24) Answer: C. "Urea is a manufactured substance based on liquid content that can come from either solid animal waste or from liquid animal waste. When cleaned and dried, it can be turned into scent-free pellets which will remain unfrozen down to temperatures of 18°C. After all, who's ever seen an elephant slip? Certainly not me!" said Flo Klukis of the Liverpool City Council.

25) Answer: Think about. The researchers divided test subjects into three groups, asking one to imagine moving their pinky, another to imagine using their elbow muscles, and the last to imagine nothing at all—and to do this 15 minutes a day, 5 days a week, for 12 weeks. Muscular strength in the relevant areas increased noticeably in to the two "think-method" groups, and not at all in the lazy good-for-nothings.

26) Answer: Beauty. MIT and Harvard researchers found that the brain's response to beautiful women triggered the same reward circuits in the brain as food. Study author Hans Breiter claims that his is the first study to show that the response to feminine beauty is hardwired, not socially conditioned. In the experiment, pictures of women were flashed before men who were wired to neuroimaging equipment. The men worked frantically to keep the beautiful women on the screen, each pressing the keyboard thousands of times in the 40-minute session. Said Breiter, "These guys look like rodents pressing the bar for cocaine."

27) Answer: Cell phones. The *London Telegraph* reports that Stealth aircraft can be easily traced by the antenna networks used to transmit cell phone calls. Cell phone calls bounce between antennae that produce a screen of radiation that is disrupted by the Stealth planes. Thus, the next time your cell phone rings unexpectedly, throw a rock straight up as hard as you can, and you never know what might come down.

28) Answer: A. Equipped with magic wand and tutu, the Wish Fairy visited Tupperware sales meetings and granted the deepest wish and valuable prizes to chosen hostesses.

29) Answer: Space. NASA has included do-it-yourself pregnancy tests in medical packs bound for the international space station. This adds some credibility to the rumored existence of an exclusive 200 Mile-High Club, but as the late NASA technician Harry Stine detailed in his book *Living in Space*, such celestial trysts may not be all that romantic. Stine says NASA conducted some research in a buoyancy tank and discovered, "It was possible but difficult and was made easier when a third person assisted by holding one of the others in place."

30) Answer: Lint. What the heck is belly button lint? Australian physicist Karl Kruszelnicki enlisted the help of 5,000 people who conducted various belly button experiments on themselves. Among their discoveries: Rather than descending from the shirt or sweater, most belly button lint is carried upward by hairs from the underwear. Referencing the key role of body hair, Kruszelnicki concludes, "Hairy, overweight men produce more fluff than slim, hairless women."

31) Answer: Crunchy. Soggy cornflakes will be one more thing we have to explain to our incredulous grandchildren if the folks at the biotech company Monsanto have their way. Monsanto specializes in genetically modified foods and is looking to create a strain of Super Corn, which, injected with the genes of wax-producing plants, will give cornflakes a built-in shield against the mush-making influence of milk. The environmental organization Friends of the Earth told London's *Daily Telegraph*, "This has a fair claim to be the most pointless genetically modified product yet."

32) Answer: Tongue. A Brazilian company has created an electronic tongue to replace human food and drink tasters. The journal *Nature* reports that the handheld device can be used to detect impurities in water and is sophisticated enough to distinguish between different vintages of wine from the same vineyard.

33) Answer: A. "When you lie, you feel guilty about it, and along with this guilt, an increase in adrenalin is released and the adrenalin causes your blood pressure to go up and your pulse rate to go up, which is what we measure with a lie detector," said Dr. Alan Hirsch of the Smell and Taste Foundation of Chicago, discussing the Pinocchio Effect.

34) Answer: Michael Turner, describing the sound of the Big Bang. Three groups of scientists recently presented their case that the universe began with low tones they call the "music of creation." Among the aftereffects of the Big Bang were these tones, which still echo through the cosmos. In fact, they're part of the static in your TV.

35) Answer: A. Pam Teflon, the drag queen. More recently, one of the top-selling salespeople in Los Angeles is Phranc (sounds like Frank), a noted lesbian folksinger.

Stupid Criminals

1) Answer: In uniform and in a marked car. Gabriel Lajoye will be inducted into the Stupid Criminals Hall of Fame for trying to buy 56 grams of cocaine from a uniformed Carmel, Indiana, police officer, in his marked patrol car, in a public parking lot, in broad daylight. The *Indianapolis Star* says the suspect told a police officer he knew that if the cop ran into large amounts of cocaine in the course of his duties, Lajoye could take it off his hands. The cop set up Mr. Lajoye, who happily obliged.

2) Answer: Squeezing and poking baked goods. Samuel Feldman denied he prodded biscuits and poked bread loaves, destroying them in the process. But in-store cameras caught the baked goods handler. In court he admitted, "I do touch bread too much, yes, much more than the next person."

3) Answer: Parade. Wells' annual holiday parade was underway when a man, who had been drinking while watching the parade, got into his car and joined it. He cruised around the floats and marching bands until the chief of police—who happened to be leading the parade—stepped in front of the car and flagged him down.

4) Answer: A Whopper . . . with cheese. The man brandished a gun in a Manchester, Connecticut, Burger King and forced the staff to get into the walk-in freezer. After getting the manager to open the safe and fork over the store's cash, the robber took the manager to the freezer, ordered the fry cook out, and demanded that he cook up a Whopper. Said a policeman, "That order was to go."

5) Answer: Told the holdup guy to "get out." Akron police are looking for the man who entered a local bank, handed the teller a note demanding money, and then took his note and left when the teller said, "Get out." Supervisors at the bank say the teller did not handle the situation properly and are schooling her on the proper steps to take during a holdup.

6) Answer: Plunger. The station attendant says he wasn't scared when a man walked in with a toilet plunger stuffed under his coat. The robber pretended it was a gun, but the attendant wasn't fooled. When the robber demanded money, the attendant just said, "No." The robber turned and ran, dropping his "weapon." He was later arrested.

7) Answer: Comb-over. Look out America, the Comb-Over Bandit is still on the loose. According to police in California, a white man in his late forties successfully robbed the same bank teller on two consecutive Tuesdays. Investigators branded him the Comb-Over Bandit in reference to his hair, which the *Los Angeles Times* described as, "apparently styled to cover a bald patch." Said FBI agent Julie McWilliams, "That was the first thing that everybody noticed about him."

8) Answer: Waiter. Donald Allen Batman was a former waiter, so he knew the drill. He would enter Reno, Nevada, restaurants, act like an employee, ask people if he could take their payments, and then abscond with the money. He got more than $200 before he was arrested. The judge in the case told Mr. Batman, "Holy guacamole, that was pretty clever what you did." He then added, "pretty stupid, too."

9) Answer: Doing a cartwheel. Ohio patrolman Joseph Kapronica saw a van veering out of control and pulled over 42-year-old Nancy Lang, who flat out told him, "Give me a break. I'm drunk." After she failed to stand on one leg or walk heel to toe, however, Lang told Kapronica, "Wait, I can do this." ("This" being five jumping jacks, one pushup, and an attempted cartwheel.) Concerned "for her safety and mine," Kapronica stopped Lang and arrested her on several charges.

10) Answer: Dog biscuits. Doras Lamar Campbell Jr. of Georgetown walked into the store and asked where the dog section was. Then, with his hand in his jacket in a gunlike fashion, he told the clerk, "Don't make me do this." Campbell ran out of the store with the hot dog biscuits and hopped on his getaway bike. Someone called the cops. A short chase ensued and Campbell was apprehended. It has not been determined for whom the goods were ultimately destined.

11) Answer: 13 pigs.

12) Answer: By his car. Scott Knight's Chevy Tahoe features the big automotive status symbol, On-Star, which uses satellites and wireless technology to provide assistance and information to drivers. According to ABC News, On-Star alerted Merced, California, police after Knight's airbag deployed. It reported the exact location and a detailed description of the car. When police arrived, they found a 24-year-old motorist who had been struck by a hit-and-run driver. Police used the low-tech method of following a trail of leaked fluid to locate and arrest Knight.

13) Answer: Starbuck's tip jar. Candidate Joey Racano of Surf City claimed he was "only making change" after customers reported seeing him with his hand in the jar. Nevertheless, Racano was arrested on suspicion of taking money. The candidate blames his arrest on his prominent anti-Starbucks activism. He has been protesting the coffee store for using milk from cows injected with bovine growth hormone. Said Racano "The bottom line is they want me out of town."

14) Answer: Census worker. Hubert Lambert was quite passionate about his job; so much so that when a woman didn't come to the door he decided to just walk into her house and leave the questionnaire on her table. Lambert's persistent knocking and ringing also scared a 14-year old girl who was home alone watching TV. "I went into the kitchen because I didn't want him to see me," she said. In his own defense, Mr. Lambert claimed that he was never trained how to handle such situations. "We were left to our own devices to get our forms filled out."

15) Answer: Snack foods. Police in Ashtabula, Ohio, found the snack thief asleep in his car surrounded by cookies, chips, and beef jerky, and charged him with grand larceny. The unidentified suspect claimed that he and a 16-year-old accomplice drove to a Frito Lay distribution center, found an unlocked delivery truck, and just helped themselves.

16) Answer: Get free food. Jeremy Henthorn told restaurant owners in Knox County, Ohio, that he was with the Ohio State Patrol. And they responded by feeding him for free. Interestingly, he did this without either a uniform or a badge. The highway patrol believes the scam worked at least 20 times, although none of the restaurants would confirm it.

17) Answer: School exams. They were looking for two other bags filled with money, more than half a million dollars. But hey, they were in a hurry. So now they have students' exam papers in Latin, algebra, and chemistry.

18) Answer: Overdue books. Apparently, they know how to deal with library scofflaws in Mapleton, Minnesota. Leroy Anderson was confronted by police for the two books he had checked out in 1999 and then forgotten. Even more embarrassing than the nature of the crime was that the local paper announced the titles of the books in question: *A Woman of Passion* and *Secret Obsession*.

19) Answer: Renovated. Arthur Jacobs drove up to his summer home in Vermont to discover a young couple repainting the walls. They had sold various antiques in the house to pay for the paint and other, more extensive renovations, including new plumbing. The couple told police that they "believed in communal property and sharing." They were charged with burglary and trespassing.

20) Answer: Marijuana plants. Police got a call from Emmit Scott, complaining of assault. He told them that a young man had attacked him and taken some of his marijuana plants. He then showed police his garden, which still had 27 plants. The biggest marijuana bust in Halifax County history.

21) Answer: Dewey, Cheatham, and Howe. For years, Patrick Michael Penker used the name of the Three Stooges fictional law firm to obtain cashier's checks from banks in Lubbock. Eventually, banker John Reed from American State Bank became suspicious and called the FBI. "It did seem just a bit unusual for a company name," said Reed. Penker has pleaded guilty to charges including identity fraud and money laundering.

22) Answer: A walk in the woods. The *Cleveland Plain Dealer* reported that Judge Michael Cicconetti gave Kenyata Reid two choices: 2 days in jail or 3 hours alone in the woods. The judge wanted Reid to understand the benefits of silence. Reid says the time alone did help him see the error of his ways.

23) Answer: A teddy bear. Firefighters were called to the home of Lucson Aladin because of a reported brush fire. Instead, they found a teddy bear aflame. Aladin told the firefighters that he ignited the bear because it was possessed. He was charged with reckless burning.

24) Answer: Living with and having sex with. A judge convicted Jerry Ward of "living in sin" with his girlfriend, citing North Carolina's 1805 adultery law. Ward admitted to cohabitating with his girlfriend, Wendy Gunter. He was ordered to pay for court costs incurred during the trial. The law, enforced by district judge and ordained minister Jimmy Myers, strictly prohibits unmarried couples to "lewdly and lasciviously associate, bed and cohabit together."

25) Answer: An hour-long walk down Main Street in a dress. Proving once again that Ohio law enforcement has a sense of humor, Jason Householder and John Stockum chose the promenade down Main Street Coshocton in tasteful frocks with wigs and makeup. The two men were arrested for denting a car with beer bottles and insulting a woman. Says Judge David Hostetler of the punishment, "I've got a jail with 52 people that's supposed to hold 36 . . . you run out of options."

26) Answer: Fugitive. Richard Hansen was walking around San Diego wearing an orange shirt with the word FUGITIVE printed on it—arousing the suspicion of local police officers. After officer Laura Tosatto stopped Hansen, she checked his record and found that he actually was a fugitive. "It doesn't get much easier," said Lieutenant Ken Franke.

27) Answer: 44 birds in his pants. Carlos Rodriguez Avila was charged with illegal importation and possession of birds after he arrived on a charter flight from Havana, Cuba. Apparently, the jig was up when he went through Customs and was asked to raise his pant legs. Inspectors saw something strapped to his legs; they widened their search and inevitably found 44 melodious Cuban finches in his pants.

28) Answer: Ignored. The three masked men appeared in a Belgian bowling hall and began loudly demanding money while brandishing rifles. The staff was so busy serving drinks to the 100 or so people in attendance that they didn't realize what was happening. Frustrated, the potential thieves left. Said one employee, "It was only after they left and one visitor asked us why they had weapons that we realized they were robbers."

29) Answer: Breast implants. The police Breathalyzer technician claimed that Donna Pringle only pretended to blow air while being administered the test. Pringle's defense: She was unable to blow harder because of recent breast-augmentation surgery. And it worked; the court overturned her conviction due to a lack of proof that Pringle deliberately tried to deceive the Breathalyzer.

30) Answer: Going on a beer run. Said Jim Donnon, the facility superintendent, "He wiggled through a little tiny crack in the fence. He's a little fellow." Once outside the St. Johnsbury County work camp, prisoner Mark Delude walked to the nearest convenience store where he bought a carton of smokes, a case of Bud, and a 40-ounce, which he enjoyed during the return trip. He was busted on his return. "When he's sober he's a great worker," Donnon said of the inmate. "But these guys aren't known for making good decisions."

31) Answer: Boat. Nobody's ever attempted to rob a bank on the Aland Islands, west of mainland Finland, because there's no place to get away to. The islands are tiny and everybody knows everybody else anyway. The robber didn't have any way to get off the island, so police apprehended him within minutes, presumably after he stuck his toe in the Baltic Sea and went, "Brrrr!"

32) Answer: Remotes. Jaron Grosby and Wesley Jackson were spotted leaving a house carrying two television sets through a broken window. They would have gotten away clean but they went back into the house to fetch the remotes. By the time they retrieved them and got back to their car, the police had arrived.

33) Answer: The fire chief and bragged about it. Twenty-year-old Nichols Breidenstein torched a doughnut shop then tried to phone his cohort, 21-year-old Michael Bannister. When someone answered the call, Breidenstein said, "Dude, it's lit! The whole corner's going." Unfortunately, the arsonist called the wrong number and got fire chief Michael Guadagno at home. The fire chief said,

"He's probably got a better chance of winning the lottery than dialing the wrong number and getting the fire chief again."

34) Answer: Prison. Mr. Monas is serving a prison term for unrelated fraud and forgery charges, but he used the pay phone in the prison common room to call employees and clients and convince them to give him their money. According to the AP, to explain his irregular schedule and the strange ambient sound, he often said he was calling from Europe or a crowded restaurant. Some clients became concerned about their investments when they received handwritten receipts.

35) Answer: Résumé. Scot Alan Beane, 37, accidentally dropped his own résumé at a bank while robbing it—5 days after he robbed another bank and left a receipt with his name on it. Unsurprisingly, he had been drinking. Says a police spokesman, "Here's the story—you shouldn't drink and drive. You shouldn't rob banks, either."

36) Answer: Another prison. Arnold Ancheta used a mop handle and a bed sheet to climb onto the roof and then get over the fence, but instead of jumping over the fence that led to a public road, he jumped the smaller fence that guarded the neighboring women's prison. He was spotted running around the women's prison yard—presumably giving himself repeated dope-slaps—and was quickly re-apprehended.

37) Answer: Laundry. Employees at a dry cleaner in Murfreesboro, Tennessee, found the note among some shirts that were brought in to be laundered. They immediately called the FBI, which confirmed that one of the shirts, a black number with white pinstripes, matched the description of a shirt worn by a bank robbery suspect. He was quickly arrested and charged with three counts of robbery.

38) Answer: Potato. Alpha McQueen pointed a gun at three women in an argument about money from a drug deal. No shots were fired, but Mr. McQueen had stuck a potato on the end of his gun. Prosecutors said he was attempting to use the potato as a silencer, and silencers are illegal under federal law. In fact, using one in a drug crime carries a 25-year mandatory sentence.

That will be more than twice the sentence of his accomplice, who used no potato.

39) Answer: Invisible. Leon Joseph Clemons was arrested while walking down the street naked. He was accused of robbing from the store where he worked and stealing a car and a dog—he liberated a Shih-Tzu, worth about $300, from its locked kennel. He told police that he took off his clothes so they couldn't see him. Police told him that it didn't work.

40) Answer: Peanut butter sandwich. Joy Dubord says she was arguing with Sandra Guba over the affections of the massage therapist they both loved, when, "She shoved me and hit me in the side of the head with a peanut butter sandwich. When I went out of the house I still had it on the side of my head where she pounded it." Guba claims that she merely sprinkled crumbs on Dubord's head and charged that Dubord smeared peanut butter on herself to enhance the case.

41) Answer: Induces labor. The four men thought they had gotten a hold of OxyContin, a drug that, when snorted, gives a heroin-like high. They were close, but if they looked more closely they would've seen that they had grabbed Oxytocin, a drug that induces childbirth, aids lactation, and, some say, fosters mothering instincts. "They're not very smart," said sergeant Eddie Moore, leading to more than one news organization referring to the thieves as oxy-morons.

42) Answer: Committed a crime. After checking "yes," Edwin V. Gaynor told officers that he had carjacked a woman and robbed five people in Texas. Obviously, people who already had jobs in law enforcement promptly arrested him. He even provided police with a few details about the crime, telling them about his chrome-plated handgun and green-and-white bandanna.

43) Answer: Cut eyeholes in their masks. The *Daily Star* reported that the two robbers were captured on closed-circuit TV with wool hats pulled over their faces, stumbling around the news shop they were trying to rob, bumping into counters while the store owners called the police. The two robbers then pulled the masks up and their faces were caught on camera. They were arrested shortly after their crime, having stolen three packs of cigarettes. The videotape was played at their trial. Lawyers for both sides could barely contain their amusement.

44) Answer: A ham. One free Easter giveaway ham, to be exact—available to Ralph's shoppers who had spent $50 or more on other groceries. Rachel Cheroti arrived at the checkout lane with $48 worth of groceries and demanded a ham, which she got. But she became upset when the manager refused to give her more than one, and pinned him against the wall with her cart when he tried to escort her from the store. They grappled on the floor while another shopper and a policeman tried to intervene. The policeman tore some ligaments in his hand. Cheroti was arrested on battery charges.

Miscellaneous

1) Answer: A. "I don't know if waving those brightly colored wand things and pretending that you're Obi Wan Kenobi is exactly what it means to be a Jedi. I think you need to do slightly more than fill in 'Jedi' on your census form," said Joanne Black, reporter for *The Evening Post* in Wellington, New Zealand.

2) Answer: C. As the Poison Squad ate more borax, they got sicker and sicker, and Dr. Wiley suggested that Congress ban borax in food. Since then, it's mainly been used as a cleaning agent.

3) Answer. A. The Bostwick consistometer is a device used to accurately measure the viscosity of food products.

4) Answer: C. Mr. Dichter, known as the founder of motivational psychology, once also wrote—admittedly in the 1940s—that people liked to smoke cigarettes because they enjoyed watching the smoke.

5) Answer: B. "The facial features are not recognizable, and the body is not recognizable because, as I recall, just before his death, Sonny Bono was a much heavier man than the one described in this statue. This statue is of a man that has a 28-inch waist, and we know that Sonny Bono did not have a 28-inch waist," said Dario Jones, who operates a gallery near the statue in Palm Springs.

6) Answer: C. Examples are "That wave was crispy, or crunchy, hearty, tasty, sweet, etc."

7) Answer: A. A Clinton wave.

8) Answer: A. Talking to the seals. A noun form is called the aqua boot.

9) Answer: Women's panties. A man in Fallon, Nevada, received a package with no return address. He opened it and found unsigned love letters and women's black-lace panties. He turned the package over to sheriff's deputies saying that he just moved to town and few people knew his address. He became

worried about anthrax poisoning because he sniffed the contents to determine if they were perfumed. A local woman admitted sending him the letter and panties, saying it was a romantic overture to the new man in town.

10) Answer: Loaded his plate with food. Fire officers say other patrons stole tips from tables or disappeared without paying their bills. One diner asked whether the restaurant would reopen later so she could have her pudding.

11) Answer: Too mean. The 57-year-old Slaughter has a bad reputation in Richford. He apparently is so abusive that even his family refused to save him from the fire. Volunteer firefighters said the same thing. Two state troopers finally got him out of the house.

12) Answer: A. "Many of them want to have the fat taken out of the double-chin area, but most of them want to have more projection of the chin because they feel that it offers an appearance of someone who is more in the know and more confident," says Steven Anderson, a plastic surgeon in the Seattle area.

13) Answer: Stroke. Scientists at the University of Pennsylvania have found that some plants may indeed grow faster and become more resistant to disease and insects if stroked, very carefully, at least once a week. One group of houseplants were given one stroke, from stem to tip, once a week while other groups were denied such attention. Not all the plants responded favorably, but researchers say the study provided important clues to how living things respond to contact with one another.

14) Answer: Spoiled. An Italian psychotherapist has confirmed what was long suspected—our bosses are just grown-up brats. After interviewing 300 managers, Serenella Salomoni determined that the majority of bosses were spoiled by their parents as children and grew up with an inflated sense of self. She says, "Their success comes from being pushed by their families. They live with the idea that they are the best at whatever they do and being told they are the smartest or the prettiest."

15) Answer: B. Walter Fleming was a Mason—a member of a fraternal society that goes back 300 years—and he was sitting around with other Masons talking about how boring things were. Another member, an actor, had just seen a play

in Europe with colorful oriental costumes. Using this for inspiration, the Shriners were born.

16) Answer: B. In 1991, an inductee in Louisville sued the organization, saying that he passed out from the stress of the ritual and that the Shriners then stuffed whipped cream and strawberries in his shorts. The suit was thrown out.

17) Answer: A. The Cup O' Justice Cafe lists varieties of legal advice and prices on its blackboard menu, next to the beverages. The advice is dispensed by the owner, Jim Skelton, a graduate of the University of North Dakota Law School.

18) Answer: A. "He's lucky that we didn't know about his double life then, I mean, you know, wearing a dress . . . very interesting," says Nick Meglin, co-editor of *Mad* magazine, speaking of his magazine's troubles with J. Edgar Hoover.

19) Answer: Condom machines. The machines were sent to the research base on the Ross ice shelf. According to the vendor, Kevin Ashton, "It's pretty much a little village where everyone knows everyone, so if they walk into a loo to buy a condom it's a lot more comfortable than going to the local shop and buying them when everyone knows what's going on." More than 1,500 people work there in the summer versus fewer than 50 during the winter.

20) Answer: New Porsche dealership. Lynch Porsche on Chicago's North Side is the city's first Porsche dealership and probably the first anywhere to be blessed by a cardinal. Cardinal George says he was responding to a request from his old friend, a car dealer who provides him with his official car, which, by the way, is a Buick LeSabre. The Cardinal finished his blessing with the traditional splashing of holy water onto the hood of a 2001 Porsche Boxster priced at $63,000.

21) Answer: Tobacco. The *New York Times* reported that restaurants in Manhattan have started adding tobacco to their dessert sauces and as a garnish—even though smoking tobacco is illegal in New York restaurants. Says Chef Bernard Dance, "For a chef it's important to always do something new, and to provoke people." The taste of tobacco is described by the *Times* as haunting, with an oak-aged spirit, notes of leather, and wet earth.

22) Answer: Stink bomb. The technical problems of trying to perfect such a bomb are many—odors are culturally learned, so what stinks to us might not to some foreign enemy, and people become accustomed to most bad odors within 15 minutes or so. So far, the best solution has been a variation on a World War II formulation that approximates the scent of human waste and was called "Who, me?" A scientist working on the project says that "Who, me?" was designed to be sprayed on German officers by the French Resistance. She says, "This, of course, would totally embarrass the officer, causing Germany to lose the war."

23) Answer: Your spouse. Even if you don't like them, your blood pressure will still go down. This is according to assistant professor of psychology Brooks Gump of the State University of New York at Oswego. Gump is the lead author of a study that suggests that the drop in blood pressure has more to do with the predictable patterns of spousal relationships and less to do with the pleasure we derive from such relations.

24) Answer: Stuck. Dutch contortionist Berkine experienced a rubber man's worst nightmare while warming up before his act—his left foot got stuck behind his neck. Even worse, his circus pals ignored his cries for help because they thought he was joking. After some good-natured ribbing, they realized he was serious and immediately went to find a local doctor. Dr. Harinder Gowal quickly freed Berkine, who said he had "terrible pins and needles for ages afterwards."

25) Answer: An unidentified student at Beverly Hills High School. The student was complaining to a reporter about the smelly oil well situated right next to the school. Long before it became famous for entertainment and plastic surgery, Los Angeles was a center for the oil industry. Once upon a time, there were 3,000 active oil wells in the Los Angeles basin. Many of the oil wells are still there, but disguised. The well next to Beverly Hills High School is camouflaged by 15 stories of vinyl flowers.

26) Answer: A. "Lydia's most excited about early versions of AOL disks, so she traded away one of her modern AOL disks that had a picture of Alfred E. Newman from *Mad* magazine for an early version of AOL. She was quite excited about that trade," says Tim Higgins of the *Kansas City Star*.

27) Answer: Hands. Word out of the University of Chicago is that gesticulating madly with your hands makes you smarter. In a study, researcher Susan Goldin-Meadow and colleagues found that people who used their hands to explain something had an easier time remembering things. How does this work? Goldin-Meadow says, "We don't really know. I would say, gesture up a storm. It can't hurt you."

28) Answer: D'oh! That's right, D'oh. Homer Simpson's way of expressing regret at his own stupidity is now officially good English. Dan Castellenetta, the voice of Homer Simpson, told us that he stole the expression from a character in old Laurel and Hardy films, who would say, when frustrated, "D'o-o-o-o-o-o-o-oh!" When told that there wasn't time for such a long exclamation in the early *Simpsons* shorts, he shortened it to "D'oh!"

29) Answer: Alpha pups, or cool kids. Alpha pups are the kids you looked up to in grade school, and Hasbro hopes to tap into their influence to sell new electronic games. To find these Type-A adolescents, market researchers combed arcades and skate parks looking for boys between the ages of 8 and 12, asking them, "Who is the coolest kid you know?" Then they would find that kid and ask him the same question. When some cocky kid finally said, "Me," they knew they had found their pup and offered him $30 to learn to play their new game and tell his friends about it.

30) Answer: Acne. Thanks to his pimply teenaged skin, 14-year-old Pierce Nahigyan of Irvine, California, was deemed an unacceptable health risk by his mother's health insurer. She had tried to enroll her three children together, but because Pierce had once been treated for acne, he was disqualified for having a preexisting condition.

31) Answer: B. "We have a patented nozzle. It's clinical and rotates and projects a lot of little drops of water at a high speed—that's what provides the massage, but it also has enough power to remove the dirt without removing the natural oil coating of the pet," says Andre Diaz, co-inventor of the Lavakon pet-washing machine.

32) Answer: Robert Parker, who has been deemed the most influential wine critic in the world. What does he review? Parker, according to the

Washington Post, is a "gluttonous, wine-swigging middle-age guy who lives in Maryland." He publishes *The Wine Advocate*, and his power to make or break a cabernet has given him influence that movie and book critics would kill to have. He's particularly hard on French pomposity. He's been sued by Bordeaux winemakers and once was attacked by an irate vineyard owner's dog.

33) Answer: Get some doughnuts. While on a routine patrol of the city, an officer and the pilot made a quick landing at a local Krispy Kreme doughnut shop. Lieutenant Bob Huntsman of the Albuquerque Police Department says, "We've worked too hard, too long to make this a professional unit to let one lapse screw it up for us. On top of that, it doesn't do much for the cops and doughnuts stereotype."

34) Answer: A snowman. Bob Bowling first told Clark County police that he shot himself when his gun went off in his holster while sitting down. But when pressed, he admitted that he was practicing his quick draw against a frozen opponent in his back yard. Bowling was released after receiving medical treatment and widespread mockery. The snowman is still at large, though it hasn't moved.

Acknowledgments

When you come up with an idea for a radio show, it turns out you're about 10% of the way to actually making one. An amusing news quiz featuring fabulous, witty panelists seemed like a natural for NPR back in, oh, 1994 or so. Years later, when it finally launched in January 1998, it had already gone through three iterations and countless turn-arounds, tweaks, and tryouts.

The first pilot, in 1995, was, in retrospect, very news heavy. It was also about 2½ hours long (hey, what did we know? We were terrified we'd run out of material). It was produced at NPR in Washington with a team of young news veterans. It was hosted by then–Talk of the Nation host (and now NewsHour Trivia Question) Ray Suarez. It featured panelists such as Pentagon Correspondent Martha Raddatz, and *Washington Post* Tokyo Bureau Chief T. R. Reid. The verdict was that the content was worthy of NPR, but not yet enough fun for the weekend. We tried again in New York City a couple of years later. This time we de-emphasized news and concentrated on humor. Our host was the talented *New York Times* "Ethicist" Randy Cohen, and our panelists were a group of great New York writers. When the reviews came in, however, it was a bit too light. What NPR listeners wanted was fun *with* substance. They wanted to learn something *while* laughing. That delicate balance is what we aimed for in our third and final pilot attempt in 1997. It worked. With just enough success to get by on, we launched the show in January of 1998, more or less in the form you hear it now on your local NPR station. We are immensely grateful to all the people who helped us get that far and to all the NPR stations that feature us on their air.

Since that 1998 debut, our own staff and panelists (whose introductions to chapters you've read) have pushed to continually reinvent, modify, and improve the show. That's as it should be. We try to surprise and delight each other with new ideas and new ways to play with the week's news. We figure if we're laughing, you'll be laughing. Each week's show is a matter of scouring news sources worldwide, and then throwing an awful lot of material up against the wall. What you've read in this book was the stuff that stuck. It was all found, flung, and made acceptable for human consumption by our fun and talented staff: Senior Producer Rod Abid; Host Peter Sagal; Official Judge and Score-keeper Carl Kasell; producers Diantha Parker, Michael Danforth, and Amanda Gibson as well as Technical Directors Lorna White and Robert Neuhaus. Our Listener Limerick Challenge was created by Leslie Fuller, and her tradition is carried on by our current Director of Limerick Science, Philipp Goedicke. Our founding Senior Producer, who got the whole project off the ground, was David Greene. I will be forever in all of their debt (which, when you think about it, means I will never repay them. Tough luck, guys).

We also owe thanks, for inspiration, criticism, great performances, and support to the following people who played a role in the success of *Wait, Wait . . . Don't Tell Me!*:

Elizabeth Blair, Roy Blount Jr., Ariel Caminar, Jean Cochran, Randy Cohen, Sue Ellicott, Adam Felber, Corey Flintoff, Nick Gibson, Mark Greenhouse, Murray Horwitz, Peter Jablow, Troy Juliar, Mark Katz, the late Margo Kaufman, Brad Klein, Kevin Klose, Jenny Lawhorn, Joyce MacDonald, Torey Malatia, Kee Malesky, Steve O'Donnell, P. J. O'Rourke, Charlie Pierce, Martha Raddatz, Sandra Rattley, T. R. Reid, Joe Richman, Roxanne Roberts, Emmy Rubin, Michael Schweppe, Robert Siegel, Susan Stamberg, Necola Deskins Staples, Ken Stern, Ray Suarez, Jimmy Tingle, Andy Trudeau, Wesley Weissberg, Colleen Werthman, Bob Weston, and Alice Winkler, and all of the "Not My Job" guests who have been kind enough to appear on our show and risk mild humiliation over the years.

Doug Berman, Creator and Executive Producer of *WWDTM*